本书获泉州信息工程学院出版基金资助

《道德经》解读（汉英对照）

陈建平 著

Chinese-English Interpretation of *Dao De Jing*

老子智慧

The Wisdom of Laozi

苏州大学出版社
Soochow University Press

图书在版编目(CIP)数据

《道德经》解读 = Chinese-English Interpretation of Dao De Jing：汉英对照／陈建平著. --苏州：苏州大学出版社，2025.6. -- ISBN 978-7-5672-5285-1

Ⅰ. B223.15

中国国家版本馆 CIP 数据核字第 2025PJ7574 号

书　　名：《道德经》解读（汉英对照）
Chinese-English Interpretation of *Dao De Jing*

著　　者：陈建平
策划编辑：汤定军
责任编辑：汤定军
封面设计：吴　钰

出版发行：苏州大学出版社（Soochow University Press）
地　　址：苏州市十梓街 1 号　**邮编**：215006
印　　装：广东虎彩云印刷有限公司
网　　址：http://www.sudapress.com
邮　　箱：sdcbs@suda.edu.cn
邮购热线：0512-67480030
销售热线：0512-67481020

开　　本：700 mm × 1 000 mm　1/16　**印张**：16.25　**字数**：275 千
版　　次：2025 年 6 月第 1 版
印　　次：2025 年 6 月第 1 次印刷
书　　号：ISBN 978-7-5672-5285-1
定　　价：78.00 元

前言

德国哲学家卡尔·雅斯贝尔斯在其1949年出版的代表作《论历史的起源与目标》中首次提出了“轴心时代”（公元前800—前200年）这一核心概念。该术语指人类文明史上首个系统性哲学突破集中涌现的关键时期。在此期间，古希腊的苏格拉底、柏拉图、亚里士多德，古印度的释迦牟尼（佛陀），波斯的琐罗亚斯德，以及中国先秦的老子、孔子等思想先驱，以独立于神话思维的理性探索，共同开启了对人类存在终极意义的追问。他们通过伦理重构与理性思辨，为后世文明奠定了不可替代的精神根基。“轴心时代”的思想遗产至今仍在塑造着人类对生命本质、自由价值与社会正义的认知范式。其蕴含的“超越性”智慧警示我们：在技术理性占据主导的当代社会，回归对精神价值的本原追问，仍是破解文明困境的关键路径。

作为“轴心时代”中国思想的杰出代表，《道德经》在人类精神星空中犹如一颗璀璨的巨星。这部由老子撰写的道家元典，虽仅五千余言，却以极简而深邃的文字，构建起涵盖宇宙论、人生论、政治哲学等多重维度的宏赡思想体系。历经两千五百多年的时光淬炼，其智慧光芒非但未被历史尘埃遮蔽，反而在当代文明语境中愈发彰显出穿透时空的思想伟力。

老子，姓李名耳，字聃，春秋时期伟大的思想家、哲学家，道家学派的创始人。他生活在周室衰微、诸侯纷争的动荡时代，在长期的史官生涯中，得以遍览古籍，洞察历史兴衰与社会百态。老子辞官归隐途中，于函谷关应关令尹喜之请，留下了震古烁今的《道德经》。

“道”与“德”是《道德经》的核心概念。“道”在老子的思想体系里是宇宙万物的根源与本体，是一种先于天地而生、超越人类感知与理解的存在。它无声无形，却又无所不在，统摄着世间万物的运行与变化。“有物混成，先天地生，寂兮寥兮，独立而不改，周行而不殆，可以为天地母”，此句便生动地描绘了“道”的神秘性和永恒性。“道”并非人类可以随意掌控或定义，它有着自己的运行法则。所谓“道法自然”，强调“道”的运行法则是自然而然，世间万物皆应顺应“道”的法则而发展。而“德”则是形而上之“道”在形而下世界的体现和作用，是“道”内在于万物之中。“道生之，德畜之”，“道”与“德”相互依存，共同构成了《道德经》的核心思想体系。

然而，《道德经》成书年代久远，在其传承过程中，诸多复杂因素导致了大量误释误译情况的出现。早期《道德经》多以竹简记录，竹简在长期保存与流传中，可能出现错置现象，使得原本连贯的文意被打乱。后人在解读时就容易因这种顺序的混乱而产生误解，难以还原老子的本意。古代并无现代完善的标点符号体系，后人在为《道德经》断句标点时，因理解角度不同，可能会出现标点错误。而不同的标点方式会赋予句子截然不同的含义，从而引发对经文的误读。注释者在解读《道德经》时，有时会不自觉地将个人观点融入其中，甚至对原文进行修改。注释者受自身所处时代、背景及个人认知局限，其修改与解读未必契合老子原意，却可能误导后世读者对经典的理解。此外，人为的疏忽或错误在传抄、印刷过程中也难以避免。抄录者可能因笔误而写错字词，印刷过程中也可能出现排版错误等，这些看似细小的错误，经过代代相传，可能逐渐积累，使后人离《道德经》的本意越来越远。

在古代，因不同学派观点的差异及学者个人认知的局限，部分解读偏离了老子的原意。例如，有人将“无为”片面理解为消极的无所作为，而忽视了老子所倡导的顺应自然规律、不强行干预的积极内涵，使得“无为”思想被误解为一种逃避现实的处世态度。到了近现代，随着中西方文化交流的日益频繁，《道德经》被大量翻译介绍到国外。但由于语言之间巨大的文化差异和思维方式的不同，翻译过程中也出现了诸多误译。比如，“道”这一概念在英文中常被译为“Way”，而“Way”所表达的较为宽泛的“道路，方法”之意，难以准确传达“道”在《道德经》中包含的“天地万物之母，世界本源，宇宙本体”等丰富而深邃的含义。这些误译误释在一定程度上阻碍了人们对《道德经》真实智慧的理解与传承。

《道德经》的智慧，似潺潺清泉，润泽着历代中国人的心灵。它启示我们顺应自然，领悟“道法自然”的真谛，在纷繁世事中寻得内心的宁静与平衡；它告诫我们居安思危，知晓“祸兮福之所倚，福兮祸之所伏”的哲理，以辩证思维看待人生起伏；它倡导我们以柔克刚，秉持“天下莫柔弱于水，而攻坚强者莫之能胜”的理念，面对强大对手时懂得运用智慧与策略。

《道德经》的影响力不仅仅局限于华夏大地。在全球化的当下，它已成为世界文化宝库中的瑰宝，吸引着无数西方学者与思想家的目光。其蕴含的深邃哲理，为解决现代社会面临的生态危机、人际关系紧张、社会治理困境等诸多问题，提供了独特而深刻的视角。

笔者在多年为中外学生英汉双语讲授《道德经》的过程中，深切感受到了学生对这部经典的浓厚兴趣及理解上的困难，也正是基于这种教学实践才深知准确解读和恰当翻译《道德经》对于传播老子智慧的重要性。本书编纂过程中主要以王弼本、河上公本等通行传世本为底本，以傅奕本、景龙碑本、范应元本等其他传世本及出土文献郭店竹简本、马王堆帛书本等为系统对比、校勘、诠释参照，借鉴和吸纳学界同人的最新研究成果，尤其是陈鼓应、安伦的校勘和研究，纠正常见的误译误释，以“文本还原、白话今译、义理阐释、简明英译”为基本维度，初步搭建起经典解读的立体框架，力求以更加准确、全面的方式解读《道德经》，还原老子智慧的本来面目。特别值得说明的是，附录部分尝试从本体论角度阐释“道”的终极实在性及本质特性，冀望通过这种学术努力，能够稍稍触及老子之“道”作为宇宙终极实在与生命价值本源的深层义理结构。

本书秉持“在历史中理解经典”的学术理念，通过多维度的阐释尝试，既努力拂去历史语义的重重尘埃，又尽力突破历代注疏的认知局限，期望能在古今对话中逐步趋近老子思想的本真形态，展现其智慧体系的丰富内涵与哲学深度。我们真诚希望读者通过本书的解读，既能在“人法地，地法天，天法道，道法自然”的智慧观照中获得精神滋养，也能从“反者道之动”的辩证思维中得到一些应对现代性困境的启示，进而在个人修养与促进社会和谐发展层面有所裨益。

让我们共同踏上这场跨越时空的精神探索之旅，在《道德经》的智慧泉眼中，尝试探寻中华文明对人类永恒命题的独特解答。愿老子智慧照亮你的道路，指引你走向和谐、宁静与圆满的人生。

岁在甲辰暮春，于清源山老君岩下完成全书终章。

陈建平

2025 年 3 月 20 日

Preface

In his magnum opus *The Origin and Goal of History* (1949), German philosopher Karl Jaspers first introduced the seminal concept of the "Axial Age" (800 – 200 BCE). This term designates a critical epoch in human civilization marked by the unprecedented concentration of systematic philosophical breakthroughs. During this period, intellectual pioneers such as Socrates, Plato, and Aristotle in ancient Greece, Siddhartha Gautama (Buddha) in ancient India, Zarathustra in Persia, and Laozi and Confucius in pre-Qin China independently initiated rational inquiries into the ultimate meaning of human existence, emancipating thought from mythological frameworks. Through ethical reconstruction and rational speculation, they collectively laid an irreplaceable spiritual foundation for subsequent civilizations. The Axial Age's intellectual legacy continues to shape humanity's epistemic paradigms regarding the essence of life, the value of freedom, and the pursuit of social justice. Its "transcendent" wisdom serves as a vital reminder that in an era dominated by technological rationality returning to primordial spiritual interrogations remains the key to resolving civilizational dilemmas.

As a preeminent representative of Chinese thought during the Axial Age, *Dao De Jing* shines like an eternally resplendent star in the constellation of human spirituality. This foundational Taoist text, penned by Laozi in just over five thousand characters, constructs a comprehensive ideological edifice spanning cosmology, existential philosophy, and political theory through its supremely concise yet profound language. Having endured over 2,500 years of historical tempering, the wisdom of *Dao De Jing* has not only withstood the test of time but has also increasingly demonstrated its transcendent intellectual might within the discourses of contemporary civilization.

Laozi, whose surname was Li, given name was Er, and style name was Dan, was a great thinker and philosopher in the Spring and Autumn Period in ancient China, and the founder of the Taoist school. He lived in a turbulent era when the Zhou Dynasty was declining and vassal states were in incessant conflicts. During his long-term career as a court historian, he had the opportunity to read numerous ancient books, observing the rise and fall of history and all aspects of society. On his way to seclusion after resigning from his official post, at the request of Yin Xi, the commander in charge of Hangu Pass, Laozi left behind this groundbreaking *Dao De Jing*.

The concepts of "Dao" and "De" are the core ideas in *Dao De Jing*. In Laozi's ideological system, "Dao" is the origin and essence of all things in the universe. It is an existence that predates the birth of Heaven and Earth and transcends human perception and understanding. It is soundless and formless, yet omnipresent, governing the operation and changes of all things in the world. The sentences "There is something that is an integrated whole, existing before Heaven and Earth. It is soundless and formless, depending on nothing and undergoing no change, moving in a cycle and never ceasing. It can be called the mother of Heaven and Earth." vividly depict the mystery and eternity of "Dao". "Dao" is beyond human control and cannot be defined by humans, for it has its own operating laws. The so-called "the law of Dao is natural" emphasizes the naturalness of "Dao", and all things in the world grow in accordance with "Dao". As for "De", it is the manifestation and function of the metaphysical "Dao" in the physical world, and it is the essence of "Dao" inherent in all things. "Dao creates all things, and De nurtures them." "Dao" and "De" are interdependent and together constitute the core ideological system of *Dao De Jing*.

However, due to the long-standing time since the completion of *Dao De*

Jing, a multitude of complex factors have led to numerous misinterpretations and mistranslations during its circulation and dissemination. In the early days, *Dao De Jing* was mostly recorded on bamboo slips. During the long-term preservation and circulation, the bamboo slips might have been misplaced, disrupting the originally coherent text. When later generations interpret it, they are likely to be misled by this disorder and find it difficult to restore Laozi's original intention. In ancient times, there was no complete punctuation system as in modern times. When later generations punctuate *Dao De Jing*, punctuation errors may occur due to different perspectives of understanding. Different punctuation methods can give sentences completely different meanings, thus causing misinterpretations of the text. When annotating *Dao De Jing*, annotators sometimes unconsciously incorporate their personal views and even modify the original text. Limited by their own times, backgrounds, and personal understandings, the modifications and interpretations of annotators may not conform to Laozi's original intention, but could mislead later readers' understanding of the classic. In addition, human negligence or errors are inevitable during the processes of transcription and printing. Copyists may make mistakes in writing words due to carelessness, and typesetting errors may also occur during printing. These seemingly minor errors, passed down from generation to generation, may gradually accumulate, making it more and more difficult for later generations to get close to the original meaning of *Dao De Jing*.

In ancient times, due to differences in viewpoints among different schools of thought and the limitations of individual scholars' understanding, some interpretations deviated from Laozi's original intention. For example, "wu-wei" (non-action) was one-sidedly understood as passive inactivity, ignoring the positive connotation of following the laws of nature and not forcibly interfering advocated by Laozi, thus making the idea of "wu-wei" (non-action) be misinterpreted as an escapist attitude towards life. In modern times, with the increasing frequency of cultural exchanges between China and the West, *Dao De Jing* has been widely translated and introduced abroad. However, due to the huge cultural differences and different ways of thinking between languages, there have been many mistranslations in the translation process. For instance, the concept of "Dao" is often translated as "Way" in English. But the relatively broad meaning of "road, method" expressed by "Way" is difficult to accurately convey the rich and profound connotations of "Dao" in *Dao De Jing*, such as the Mother of all things in Heaven and Earth, the origin of the world, and the cosmic ontology. These misinterpretations and mistranslations have, to some extent, hindered people's understanding and inheriting of the true wisdom of *Dao De Jing*.

The wisdom of *Dao De Jing* is like a gentle stream, nourishing the hearts of generations of Chinese people. It inspires us to conform to nature, understand the true meaning of "the law of Dao is natural", and find inner peace and balance amid the complexity of the world. It warns us to be vigilant in times of peace, making us aware of the philosophical principle that "misfortune is where fortune leans upon, and fortune is where misfortune lurks", and enabling us to view the ups and downs of life from a dialectical perspective. It advocates the concept of overcoming strength with softness, upholding the idea that "nothing in the world is softer and weaker than water, and yet nothing can surpass it in attacking the hard and strong", so that when facing powerful opponents, we know how to use wisdom and strategies.

The influence of *Dao De Jing* transcends national boundaries. In today's era of globalization, it has emerged as a precious gem in the world's cultural repository, commanding the attention of numerous Western scholars and thinkers. Its profound philosophy offers unique and insightful perspectives for addressing contemporary societal challenges, including ecological crises, strained human relationships, and social governance dilemmas.

Through years of teaching *Dao De Jing* bilingually to students at home and abroad, I have keenly observed both their profound fascination with this classic and the interpretive challenges they encounter. Drawing on this teaching experience, I recognize the critical importance of accurate interpretation and appropriate translation in disseminating Laozi's wisdom across cultures. In the compilation of this book, the primary base texts are the commonly transmitted versions such as Wang Bi's version and He Shanggong's version. Other transmitted versions (e. g., Fu Yi's version, the Jinglong Stele version, Fan Yingyuan's version) and excavated texts such as the Guodian bamboo slips version and Mawangdui silk texts serve as systematic points of comparison, collation, and interpretive reference. The latest research achievements in Laozi studies, especially Chen Guying's and An Lun's collation and research, are drawn upon and incorporated, and common mistranslations and misinterpretations are corrected. A multi-dimensional framework for the interpretation of the classic is tentatively constructed, consisting of "text restoration, contemporary Chinese translation, doctrinal analysis, and concise English translation". The book strives to interpret *Dao De Jing* in a more accurate and comprehensive manner and restore the true features of Laozi's wisdom. Notably, the appendix endeavors to analyze the ontological reality of "Dao" from metaphysical perspectives, aspiring to gain a glimpse into the profound structure of Laozi's "Dao" as the ultimate cosmic reality and the source of life's value.

Guided by the academic principle of "interpreting classics within their historical contexts", this book employs multi-dimensional interpretive approaches to both clarify historical semantic ambiguities and transcend the cognitive limitations of traditional commentaries. Through this diachronic dialogue, we aim to gradually approximate the authentic form of Laozi's thought and reveal the richness and philosophical depth of his intellectual system. We sincerely hope that readers will derive spiritual nourishment from passages like "Man follows the law of Earth, Earth follows the law of Heaven, Heaven follows the law of Dao, and the law of Dao is natural" while gaining dialectical insights from "Reversion is the movement of the Dao" to address modern dilemmas, thereby fostering personal cultivation and societal harmony.

Embark with us on this trans temporal spiritual journey to explore *Dao De Jing* and seek Chinese civilization's unique responses to humanity's timeless questions. May Laozi's wisdom illuminate your path and lead you to a life of natural harmony, inner tranquility, and spiritual fulfillment.

In the late spring of the Jiachen year, the final chapter of this book was completed at the foot of Laozi Rock Stature in Qingyuan Mountain.

Chen Jianping

March 20, 2025

目录
Contents

第一章

dào kě dào fēi héng dào míng kě míng fēi héng míng
道[1]可道，非恒[2]道；名可名，非恒名。

wú míng tiān dì zhī shǐ yǒu míng wàn wù zhī mǔ
无，名天地之始；有，名万物之母。[3]

gù héng wú yù yǐ guān qí miào héng yǒu yù yǐ guān qí jiào
故恒无，欲以观其妙；恒有，欲以观其徼。

cǐ liǎng zhě tóng chū ér yì míng tóng wèi zhī xuán xuán zhī yòu xuán
此两者同出而异名，同谓之玄，玄之又玄，
zhòng miào zhī mén
众妙之门。

注释

① 道：“道”是《道德经》的核心概念。“道”是天地万物之母，是世界本原和宇宙本体。“道”是形而上的存在，它无形无象，不可名状，超越了形而下的感官认知，超越了语言和概念，却支配着万物的运行与变化，是世间一切的根源与基础。“道”又具有自然、无为、柔弱、不争、循环往复等特性（详见本书附录）。而“德”则是“道”在万物中的具体体现和作用，是事物得之于“道”的内在特质，二者相互依存，共同构成《道德经》的核心思想体系。

② 恒：通行本均作“常”，主要是避汉代孝文帝刘恒的名讳。此处据竹简本、帛书本将“常”改回“恒”，以下同。

③ 无、有：王弼本等诸本从“无名”“有名”“无欲”“有欲”处断句或连读。“天下万物生于有，有生于无”（第四十章），“无”和“有”是宇宙生成论的一对重要哲学范畴，也是老子思想的主要概念，据帛书本及庄子、王安石、高亨等各家表述，此处从“无”“有”处断句。

今译

道，如果可以说出来，就不是永恒的道了；名，如果可以叫得出来，就不是永恒的名了。无，是天地的本始；有，是万物的母亲。所以，要从恒无中观照道的奥妙，要从恒有中观察道的端倪。无与有二者有同一来源，但名称不同，共同可称为玄妙。玄妙而又玄妙，是所有奥妙的门径。

英译

The Dao that can be spoken of is not the eternal Dao; the name that can be named is not the eternal name.

Non-being is the origin of Heaven and Earth; being is the Mother of all things. Therefore, the eternal non-being is where to explore the mystery of Dao; the eternal being is where to observe the manifestations of Dao. These are both from the same source but given different names, and can together be called mystery. Being the mystery of mysteries, it is the gate to all wonders.

本章主旨

本章是总纲，形而上之“道”是老子哲学的最高范畴，它超越了语言和概念，是不可言说的，具有神秘性。“道”是天地万物的根源和本始，“无”和“有”同属于“道”的范畴。

The gist of the chapter

This chapter serves as a general outline. The metaphysical Dao is the highest category in Laozi's philosophy. It transcends language and concepts, and it is ineffable and mysterious. Dao is the root and origin of all things including Heaven and Earth. Non-being and being both belong to the category of Dao.

本章启示

本章强调“道”的深奥与超越性。“道”的不可言说：真正的“道”超越了语言和概念，须通过直觉体悟；“名”的局限性：命名和概念无法完全代表事物的本质；“无”与“有”的辩证关系：“无”是源头，“有”是生成基础，二者相互依存。“道”超越二元对立。通过体悟“道”，可以探索无限的奥秘，理解宇宙的深层规律。

The enlightenment of the chapter

This chapter highlights the profoundness and transcendence of Dao. The ineffability of Dao: Dao surpasses language and concepts and requires comprehension through intuition. The limitations of names: Naming and concepts cannot fully represent the essence of things. The dialectical relationship between non-being and being: Non-being is the source, and being is the foundation of generation, and the two are interdependent. Dao transcends binary oppositions. By comprehending Dao, one can explore infinite mysteries and understand the profound laws of the universe.

第二章

tiān xià jiē zhī měi zhī wéi měi sī è yǐ jiē zhī shàn zhī wéi shàn sī bù
天下皆知美之为美，斯恶矣；皆知善之为善，斯不
shàn yǐ
善矣。

gù yǒu wú xiāng shēng nán yì xiāng chéng cháng duǎn xiāng xíng gāo
故有无相生，难易相成，长短相形[1]，高
xià xiāng yíng yīn shēng xiāng hé qián hòu xiāng suí
下相盈[2]，音声相和，前后相随。

gù guì yǐ jiàn wéi běn gāo yǐ xià wéi jī shì yǐ hóu wáng zì chēng gū
故贵以贱为本，高以下为基。是以侯王自称孤、
guǎ bù gǔ cǐ fēi yǐ jiàn wéi běn yé fēi hū gù zhì yù wú yù bù yù lù lù
寡、不毂。此非以贱为本邪？非乎？故致誉无誉，不欲碌碌
rú yù luò luò rú shí rén zhī suǒ wù wéi gū guǎ bù gǔ ér wáng gōng yǐ
如玉，洛洛如石。人之所恶，唯孤、寡、不毂，而王公以
wéi chēng gù wù huò sǔn zhī ér yì huò yì zhī ér sǔn rén zhī suǒ jiào wú
为称。故物或损之而益，或益之而损。人之所教，吾
yì jiào zhī qiáng liáng zhě bù dé qí sǐ wú jiāng yǐ wéi jiào fù
亦教之："强梁者不得其死。"吾将以为教父。[3]

shì yǐ shèng rén chǔ wú wéi zhī shì xíng bù yán zhī jiào wàn wù zuò yān
是以圣人处无为[4]之事，行不言之教，万物作焉
ér bù shǐ wéi ér bù shì gōng chéng ér fú jū fū wéi fú jū shì yǐ
而不始[5]，为而不恃，功成而弗居。夫唯弗居，是以
bù qù
不去。

注释

① 长短相形：王弼本作“长短相较”，河上公本、傅奕本等作“长短相形”，有注家考证，古时无“较”字。据陈鼓应等校勘予以校正。

② 高下相盈：通行本作“高下相倾”，疑是避汉惠帝刘盈的名讳。故据帛书本等予以校正。

③ 通行本“故贵以贱为本，高以下为基。是以侯王自称孤、寡、不毂。此非以贱为本邪？非乎？故致誉无誉，不欲碌碌如玉，洛洛如石”原在第三十九章之末，“人之所恶，唯孤、寡、不毂，而王公以为称。故物或损之而益，或益之而损。人之所教，吾亦教之：‘强梁者不得其死。’吾将以为教父”原在第四十二章，但与章节上下文文意、逻辑不相关联，疑是错简。据安伦等校勘，此处将其合并调整至本章，则文意连贯和契合。洛洛如石：此处解释为“像石头那样朴实”，也有注本将其解释为“像石头那样坚硬”。

④ 无为：老子所言“无为”，绝非教人无所事事、无所作为，实则意在劝诫众人，须遵循自然之道，莫要悖逆自然本性而强行妄为，切不可肆意行事，无端生出诸多纷扰。深层的含义是遵循万物的本性，顺势而为以达到目的。“无为”体现“自然”，是效法“自然”的真实写照。“自然”和“无为”是道的特性，老子所说的“自然”不是现代意义上的自然界，而是指事物自然而然、本来如此、本性使然的状态，即事物自然而然的存在和发展方式，没有外在的强制干预、强作妄为和强制力量。可以说，“自然”和“无为”是二位一体的。老子的自然观认为应尽量避免“有为”，即强作妄为，如“民之难治，以其上之有为，是以难治”（第七十五章）。而有人将“无为”片面理解为消极的无所作为，忽视了老子所倡导的顺应自然规律、不强行干预的积极内涵，使得“无为”思想被误解为一种逃避现实的处世态度。

⑤ 通行本在“万物作焉而不始”后还有“生而不有”一句，而帛书本、竹简本均无此句。“生而不有”指的是生长万物而不据为己有，应是“道”之所为，疑是与第五十一章错简重出，故据此校正。

今译

天下人都知道美为什么是美，丑的观念也就产生了；都知道善为什么是善，恶的观念也就产生了。

有和无相互生成，难和易相互促成，长和短相互形成，高和下相互呈现，音和声相互和谐，前和后相互相随。

因此，尊贵以卑贱为根本，高上以低下为基础。因此，侯王自称"孤""寡""不穀"。这不是把低贱当作根本吗？难道不是吗？所以至上的称誉就是没有称誉，不要追求像玉那样华丽，而要像石头那样朴实。人们所厌恶的，就是"孤""寡""不穀"，而王公却用它们来称呼自己。所以，事物有时会因减损反而得到增益，或因增益反而受到减损。人们用来教育人的，我也用来教导别人："强横的人不得好死。"我将它作为教导别人的开始。

因此，圣人以无为的方式处理世事，以不言的方式行使教化，让万物生发而不强行促始，兴作万物而不自恃己能，功业成就而不自居有功。正因为不居功，所以他的功绩不会消失。

英译

When the people under Heaven know the idea of beauty, then the idea of ugliness arises; when the people under Heaven know the idea of good, then the idea of evil arises.

Therefore, being and non-being give rise to each other; the difficult and the easy complement each other; the long and the short contrast with each other; the high and the low position each other; tone and sound harmonize each other; front and behind follow each other.

Hence the humble is the root of the noble; the low is the base of the high. That is why lords and kings call themselves "the loner", "the solitary" and "the unworthy". Is this not to acknowledge that the humble is the root of the noble? Is this not? Therefore, the highest praise is to have no praise. Do not desire to be as gorgeous as jade, but to be as simple and plain as rock. What people dislike is "the loner", "the solitary" and "the unworthy", but these are what lords and kings call themselves. Thus things are either benefited by being diminished, or diminished by being benefited. I also teach what people teach: "A violent strongman will not die his natural death." I shall make this the start of my teaching.

Therefore, the sage manages affairs by means of "wu-wei" (non-action), preaches the doctrine without words, allows all things to develop without interfering, promotes all things without relying on his ability, and achieves his aim without claiming credit for it. Just because he claims no credit, the credit will not disappear.

本章主旨

本章揭示了事物的相对性和辩证关系，如美和丑、善和恶的相对性，以及有和无、难和易、长和短、高和下、音和声、前和后等之间都是既相互对立又相互依存的关系。阐述贵贱、高下相互依存，高贵者以低贱为根基；借侯王自称，倡导统治者谦逊低调；用“物或损之而益，或益之而损”体现辩证的损益观；通过“强梁者不得其死”倡导谦逊温和的处世原则。在阐述事物辩证关系的基础上，倡导无为而治的政治理念和不言之教的教化方式，强调功成弗居的高尚品德和深远意义，为人们提供了一种看待世界和处理事务的方法，即摒弃极端、避免偏执，以无为和顺应自然的态度去应对，追求一种超越功利、和谐自然的境界。

The gist of the chapter

This chapter reveals the relativity and dialectical relationship of things such as the relativity of beauty and ugliness, good and evil, and other relative relationships between being and non-being, the difficult and the easy, the long and the short, the high and the low, tone and sound, and front and behind, that is, all things are in a relationship of mutual opposition and interdependence. On the basis of expounding the dialectical relationship between things, it advocates the concept of "wu-wei" (non-action) and the way of teaching without speech, and provides people with a way to look at the world and deal with affairs, i. e., to avoid extremes and bigotry, respond with "wu-wei" (non-action) and conform to nature.

本章启示

世间万物是相对存在的，美与丑、善与恶相互依存。重视底层基础力量，领导者关注民众需求，个人不忘出身积累；保持谦逊，不慕虚荣，注重内在品质与实际贡献；辩证看待损益，以平和心态面对得失，不因挫折或成功而走向极端；远离强横，以谦逊温和的态度待人接物，涵育品德。圣人效法自然，以无为的方式行事，不强行干预，不居功自傲。这就要求我们以辩证的眼光看待问题，追求内心的平衡与和谐，超越对立，回归道的统一性，同时保持谦逊与包容的态度。

The enlightenment of the chapter

All things are relative; beauty and ugliness, as well as good and evil, are interdependent. Value grassroots forces: leaders heed people's needs, and individuals remember origins while growing. Be humble, focus on inner integrity and real deeds. See gains and losses dialectically, stay calm, and avoid extremes. Shun arrogance, and treat others humbly to build character. Sages practice "wu-wei" (non-action), not interfering or taking pride. We must view problems dialectically, seek inner harmony, transcend opposites to return to Dao, and maintain humility and inclusiveness.

第三章

bù shàng xián shǐ mín bù zhēng bù guì nán dé zhī huò shǐ mín bù wéi
不尚贤，使民不争。不贵难得之货，使民不为
dào bù xiàn kě yù shǐ mín xīn bù luàn
盗。不见可欲，使民心不乱。

shì yǐ shèng rén zhī zhì xū qí xīn shí qí fù ruò qí zhì qiáng qí gǔ
是以圣人之治，虚其心，实其腹，弱其志，强其骨；
héng shǐ mín wú zhì wú yù shǐ fú zhì zhě bù gǎn wéi yě wéi wú wéi zé wú
恒使民无智无欲，使夫智者不敢为也。为无为，则无
bù zhì
不治。

今译

不标榜贤能，使民众不争功名。不看重稀有的财货，使民众不去偷盗。不显耀引发欲望的事物，使民众的心不被惑乱。

所以，圣人的治理，要使人心灵清净（质朴豁达）、生活安饱、野心削弱、体魄强健；常使民众没有机巧和欲念，使自作聪明的人不敢妄为。以无为的方式治理，没有什么是不可以治理的。

英译

Do not exalt the worthy, so that the people will not contend. Do not value rare goods, so that the people will not become thieves. Do not reveal desires, so that the people's hearts will not be disturbed.

Therefore, the sage's governance is to simplify the people's minds, fill the people's stomachs, weaken the people's ambitions, and strengthen the people's bodies. The people should be always kept free from cleverness and desires, so that the cunning ones will not dare to make trouble. By governing without interference, all under Heaven will be well governed.

本章主旨

这一章主要阐述了对于社会治理的理念和观点。老子提倡一种无为而治的思想，主张通过减少外界对民众不良的引导、抑制过度的欲望和竞争之心，从物质、精神等多方面去营造一种淳朴、平和、健康的社会环境，让社会自然地达到和谐有序、良好治理的状态。

The gist of the chapter

This chapter mainly expounds Laozi's ideas and views on the ideal social governance. Laozi advocated the principle of governance by wu-wei (non-action). By reducing the adverse external influences on the people, suppressing excessive desires and competitive hearts, and creating a simple, peaceful, and healthy social environment from both material and spiritual aspects, the society can naturally reach a harmonious, orderly, and well-governed state.

本章启示

本章的核心思想是“无为而治”和“少私寡欲”。在社会治理方面，倡导减少人为干预，避免政策催生过度竞争与诱惑，遵循自然规律，不过度折腾，充分发挥民众自主性。在个人修养方面，强调克制私欲，不盲目追逐名利物质，以免陷入焦虑、痛苦之中，同时保持平和心态，不被外界单一标准左右，专注于自身内在成长。

The enlightenment of the chapter

The core ideas of this chapter are "governing by non-interference" and " reducing selfishness and minimizing desires". In terms of social governance, it is advocated to reduce human intervention. Policies should avoid giving rise to excessive competition and temptation, follow the laws of nature, refrain from making unnecessary disruptions, and give full play to the autonomy of the people. Regarding personal cultivation, it emphasizes restraining selfish desires, not blindly pursuing fame, wealth, and material things so as not to fall into anxiety and pain. At the same time, one should maintain a peaceful mindset, not be influenced by a single external standard, and focus on one's own inner development and cultivation.

第四章

dào chōng ér yòng zhī huò bù yíng yuān xī si wàn wù zhī zōng zhàn
道冲，而用之或不盈。渊兮，似万物之宗①；湛
xī sì huò cún wú bù zhī shuí zhī zǐ xiàng dì zhī xiān
兮，似或存。吾不知谁之子，象帝之先。

注释

① 通行本原在“渊兮，似万物之宗”后还有“挫其锐，解其纷，和其光，同其尘”一句，但与上下文的文意和逻辑不相关联，与第五十六章重复，疑是错简重出，故据此删除。

今译

道是虚空的，但它的作用却无穷无尽。它是那么的深邃，好像是万物的宗旨；它是那么的幽隐，好像存在又好像不存在。我不知道它是谁的孩子，好像出生在天帝之前。

英译

Dao is void, yet its use is inexhaustible. It is fathomless, yet appears to be the origin of all things. It is hidden, yet seems always present. I do not know where it comes from. It seems to have appeared before God.

本章主旨

本章着重对“道”的特性和地位进行了描述。通过展现“道”的虚空却功用无尽，深邃如同万物根源，隐而不显却真实存在，以及先于天帝存在等特点，凸显了“道”的高深莫测与根本性，让人们认识到“道”是宇宙万物存在和发展的内在依据，是一种超越人们常规认知、至高无上的存在。

The gist of the chapter

This chapter mainly describes the characteristics and status of Dao. By showing that Dao is void, yet has endless functions, profound like the origin of all things, hidden but truly existing, and prior to the God, Laozi highlighted the unfathomable and fundamental nature of Dao, making people realize that Dao is the internal basis for the existence and development of all things in the universe. It is a supreme existence that surpasses human perception.

本章启示

“道”虽无形却作用无穷，是万物根源，应透过现象探寻本质规律。同时，要敬畏未知，意识到人类认知的局限性，保持探索精神。

The enlightenment of the chapter

Although Dao is intangible and void, its use is inexhaustible. It is the origin of all things. We should explore the essential laws through phenomena. At the same time, we should hold the unknown in awe, be aware of the limitations of human cognition, and maintain a spirit of exploration.

第五章

tiān dì bù rén yǐ wàn wù wéi chú gǒu shèng rén bù rén yǐ bǎi xìng
天地不仁[1]，以万物为刍狗。圣人不仁，以百姓
wéi chú gǒu
为刍狗。

tiān dì zhī jiān qí yóu tuó yuè hū xū ér bù jué dòng ér yù chū
天地之间，其犹橐籥[2]乎？虚而不屈，动而愈出。

duō yán shuò qióng bù rú shǒu zhōng
多言数穷，不如守中。

注释

① 不仁：指没有偏爱。但不少文本将其理解为“没有仁爱”（unkind），不符合老子本意。

② 橐籥：指风箱。作为重要隐喻，融合了具象（生产工具）与抽象（宇宙本体）、经验（风箱运作）与超验（道体虚无）的双重维度，其思想精髓在于揭示真正的创造力（“愈出”）源自对本体虚静的守护（“守中”），而非人为造作。

今译

天地无所偏爱，把万物当作草狗（让万物自然生长）。圣人无所偏爱，把百姓当作草狗（让百姓自然发展）。

天地之间不正像一个风箱吗？虚空但不会竭尽，越鼓动越产出。

话多（政令繁杂严苛）反而加速败亡，不如持守虚静。

英译

Heaven and Earth are impartial, and treat all things as sacrificial straw dogs. Sages are impartial, and treat all the people as sacrificial straw dogs. Is the space between Heaven and Earth just like bellows? Void yet inexhaustible, the more it moves, the more it produces.

Much talk (Dictating too much; Too many decrees) will only accelerate failure, better keep to the mean.

本章主旨

本章主要通过对天地、圣人的行为特点的阐述，传达了老子自然无为的核心思想以及虚静、少言守中的理念。

The gist of the chapter

This chapter mainly expounds the behavioral characteristics of Heaven and Earth, and the sages. This reflects Laozi's thought of naturalness and "wu-wei" (non-action), the importance of being void and stillness, and the principle of restraining from much talk and better keeping to the mean.

本章启示

一是认识自然与社会规律的客观性，天地与圣人皆平等对待万物和百姓，人们应顺应客观，领导者须公正治理；二是领悟虚与动的辩证关系，虚怀若谷蕴含潜力，积极行动方能创造价值；三是把握言语与行动的平衡，避免多言，注重实干，做事讲究分寸，不偏不倚。

The enlightenment of the chapter

Firstly, recognize the objectivity of the laws of nature and society. Both Heaven and Earth, as well as sages, treat all things and the people equally. People should conform to objectivity, and leaders need to govern impartially. Secondly, understand the dialectics of void and action. Being open-minded contains potential, and only by taking active actions can one create value. Thirdly, maintain a balance between words and deeds. Avoid much talk, focus on practical work, being measured in doing things, and be unbiased.

第六章

gǔ shén bù sǐ shì wèi xuán pìn xuán pìn zhī mén shì wèi tiān dì gēn
谷神[1]不死，是谓玄牝[2]。玄牝之门，是谓天地根。
mián mián ruò cún yòng zhī bù qín
绵绵若存，用之不勤。

注释

① 谷神：此处“谷神”是形容“道”的。据陈鼓应等校勘，“谷”形容虚空，“神”形容变化莫测、无所不应。用“谷”象征道体的虚状，用“神”比喻道生万物的绵延不绝。

② 玄牝：玄奥的母性。此处用“玄牝”形容“道”不可思议的生殖力，即创生天地万物。

今译

谷神（道）永远不会死亡（虚空的道永不消逝），这就叫作玄妙的母体。玄妙的母体的生门，就叫作天地的根源。它连绵不绝，若隐若现，作用无尽。

英译

The Valley Spirit (Dao) never dies, and is called the Mystical Female. The birth gate of the Mystical Female is called the root of Heaven and Earth. It seems to exist continuously, and its use is inexhaustible.

本章主旨

这一章着重描述了一种作为天地万物根源的、具有玄奥特性的"道"及其作用。通过对"谷神""玄牝"等概念的阐释，揭示了宇宙万物生发、存在背后有着一种幽深、虚空且永恒的力量源泉。它孕育万物，是天地的根本，虽然看似微妙、若有若无，但其作用却是无穷无尽的，体现了老子对宇宙万物起源和内在生命力的深刻思考与体悟，进一步深化了"道"作为万物根源的思想观念。

The gist of the chapter

This chapter mainly describes the mysterious characteristics of Dao that serves as the root of all things under Heaven and Earth and its functions. Through the explanations of concepts such as the "Valley Spirit" and the "Mystical Female", Laozi revealed that there is a profound, void, and eternal source of power behind the generation and existence of all things in the universe. It creates all things, and it is the origin of Heaven and Earth. Although it seems subtle and somewhat elusive, its function is endless. This reflects Laozi's profound thinking and understanding of the origin and internal vitality of all things in the universe, and further deepens the ideological concept that Dao serves as the root of all things.

本章启示

要探寻事物根源与本质，把握根本以解决问题；秉持持之以恒精神，在个人成长与事业发展上持续发力；学会顺应自然规律，做事顺势而为，不过度强求，遵循事物发展节奏。

The enlightenment of the chapter

We should explore the origins and essences of things, and grasp the fundamentals to solve problems. We should uphold the spirit of perseverance and keep making efforts in personal growth and career development. We should learn to conform to the laws of nature, act in accordance with the trend, not force things too much, and follow the law of the evolution of things.

第七章

tiān cháng dì jiǔ tiān dì suǒ yǐ néng cháng qiě jiǔ zhě yǐ qí bù zì
天长地久，天地所以能长且久者，以其不自
shēng gù néng cháng shēng
生，故能长生。

shì yǐ shèng rén hòu qí shēn ér shēn xiān wài qí shēn ér shēn cún fēi
是以圣人后其身而身先，外其身而身存。非
yǐ qí wú sī yé gù néng chéng qí sī
以其无私邪？故能成其私。

今译

天长地久。天地能够长久，是因为它们不是为了自己而生存，所以反而能够长久存在。

所以，圣人把自己放在后面，反而能领先他人；把自己置之度外，反而能保全自己。不正是因为他们无私心吗？所以反而能成全自己。

英译

Heaven and Earth are ever-lasting. The reason why Heaven and Earth are ever-lasting is that they do not exist for themselves, so they exist for a long time. Therefore, the sage places himself behind, yet finds himself in front; disregards his own life, yet remains safe. Is it not because of his selflessness that his self is accomplished?

本章主旨

本章通过天地长久存在的原因引出圣人应秉持的处世和行事态度。借助天地“不自生”却能“长生”的现象，阐述圣人效仿天地的无私，通过将自身利益后置、置之度外的做法，最终达到在众人中领先、保全自身及实现更高层次自我价值的目的，体现了一种看似矛盾实则蕴含深刻哲理的辩证思想，即无私与成其私之间的相互转化，也为人们在为人处世、自我修养、社会治理等方面提供了独特的思考角度和行为指引。

The gist of the chapter

This chapter introduces the attitude that the sage should uphold in his life and work by citing the reasons for the eternal existence of Heaven and Earth. By referring to the phenomenon that Heaven and Earth do not exist for themselves but can exist for a long time, Laozi expounded that the sage should follow the selflessness of Heaven and Earth. By putting his own interests behind, he can finally achieve the goals of being in the front among the people, well preserving himself, and realizing higher-level self-values. This reflects a seemingly paradoxical but deeply philosophical dialectical thought in Daoism, that is, the mutual transformation between selflessness and accomplishing their selves, and also provides a unique perspective for thinking and behavioral guidance in aspects such as interpersonal communication, self-cultivation, and social governance.

本章启示

无私方能成就自我，天地因无私长久，人若超越私利为他人和社会奉献，或有意想不到的收获；谦逊是领导智慧，领导者关注团队福祉、身先士卒，能获成员追随；利他与利己统一，真诚利他，能赢得信任支持，保障自身利益。

The enlightenment of the chapter

Selflessness paves the way for self-fulfillment. Heaven and Earth can exist for a long time due to their selfless nature. When individuals rise above self-interest and wholeheartedly contribute to others and society, they often harvest unforeseen rewards. Humility represents a form of leadership acumen. When leaders prioritize the well-being of the team and lead by example, they are bound to win the loyalty and willing following of team members. Balancing altruism and self-interest is crucial. By acting with genuine altruism, one can cultivate trust and garner support, thereby effectively safeguarding one's own long-term interests.

第八章

shàng shàn ruò shuǐ shuǐ shàn lì wàn wù ér bù zhēng chǔ zhòng rén zhī
上 善 若 水。水 善 利 万 物 而 不 争 ，处 众 人 之
suǒ wù gù jī yú dào
所 恶，故 几 于 道。

jū shàn dì xīn shàn yuān yǔ shàn rén yán shàn xìn zhèng shàn zhì
居 善 地，心 善 渊 ，与 善 仁，言 善 信， 政 善 治，
shì shàn néng dòng shàn shí fú wéi bù zhēng gù wú yóu
事 善 能 ，动 善 时。[①]夫 唯 不 争 ，故 无 尤。

注释

① 居善地……动善时：此处将其作为“上德”“上善”之人（圣人）进行阐释。不少注本将其作为水的“七善”进行释义，作为“水德”的写状。

今译

至高的善就像水一样。水善于滋润万物却不与万物相争，总是处在众人所厌恶的地方，所以最接近于道。

（圣人如同水德的写状）居处善于选择地方，心胸善于保持沉静，待人善于真诚仁爱，说话善于诚实守信，为政善于有效治理，做事善于发挥才能，行动善于把握时机。正因为不与万物相争，所以没有怨咎。

英译

The highest good is like water. Water benefits all things without contending, and stays in places that all dislike. Therefore, it is close to Dao.

In positioning, the sage is good at keeping his place. In heart, being profound. In relations, being benevolent. In words, being faithful. In governing, being effective. In deeds, being skilled. In actions, being timely. It is just because he does not contend that he is free from reproach.

本章主旨

这一章通过对近似于“道”的水的品性剖析，将水所具备的品德与圣人（至善的人）为人处世、治理国家等联系起来，让人们更加形象地理解“道”善利万物而不争的内涵和特质，为人们提供了一套具体的、可实践的行为准则和道德规范，以此来达到一种理想的、顺遂无咎的生活和治理状态。

The gist of the chapter

Through an analysis of the character of water which is similar to Dao, this chapter connects the virtues of water with the way the sages conduct themselves in life and govern the country, enabling the people to better understand the connotation and characteristics of Dao, which benefits all things without contention, and provides people with a set of specific and practical codes of conduct and ethics, so as to achieve an ideal, smooth and guilt-free life and governance state.

本章启示

本章以“上善若水”为喻，揭示了利物不争、柔韧处下的生命智慧。水滋养万物而不居功，启示现代人在追求发展时须兼顾利他精神与生态伦理；而遇方则方、遇圆则圆的特性则教导人们在压力下保持灵活心态；甘居低处的品格则指引我们以谦逊格局超越世俗纷争。这种刚柔并济的哲学既倡导尊重自然规律的可持续发展理念，又为个体在进取与淡泊之间寻求平衡提供了东方智慧，在当代社会仍具深刻的现实意义。

The enlightenment of the chapter

This chapter uses the metaphor of " the highest good being like water" to reveal the life wisdom of benefiting without contention and adapting through humility. Water nourishes all things without claiming credit, inspiring modern people to balance altruism with ecological ethics in development; its flexibility to conform while maintaining persistence teaches resilience in the face of pressure; and its willingness to occupy lowly positions guides us to transcend worldly disputes with humility. This philosophy of integrating hardness and softness not only advocates sustainable development respecting natural laws but also offers the Oriental wisdom for individuals to balance ambition and serenity, holding profound contemporary relevance.

第九章

chí ér yíng zhī bù rú qí yǐ chuǎi ér ruì zhī bù kě cháng bǎo jīn yù
持而盈之，不如其已。揣而锐之，不可长保。金玉
mǎn táng mò zhī néng shǒu fù guì ér jiāo zì yí qí jiù gōng suì shēn tuì
满堂，莫之能守。富贵而骄，自遗其咎。功遂身退，
tiān zhī dào yě
天之道也。

今译

执持盈满，不如适可而止。锐利锋芒，不可能长久。金玉满堂，无人能守得住。富贵骄横，自己招来祸患。功业完成就隐身而退，这合于自然大道。

英译

Filling（a vessel）to the brim is not as good as stopping in due time. Sharpening a blade too much will not keep its edge for long. Filling a hall with gold and jade is impossible to keep them safe. Being wealthy and arrogant is to bring trouble upon oneself. To retire after achieving success conforms to the Dao of Heaven.

本章主旨

本章从多个方面对人们的行为处事提出了警示，通过生活中常见的追求圆满、彰显锋芒、积累财富、居功自傲等现象，告诫人们要避免过度、懂得知足、收敛锋芒、保持谦逊、适时隐退，强调了遵循自然之道

的重要性，引导人们以一种更加明智、平和且符合自然之道的方式去生活和处事。

The gist of the chapter

In this chapter, Laozi gave warnings to the people's behaviors and ways of handling affairs. Through phenomena commonly seen in life such as striving for perfection, showing off one's edge, accumulating wealth, and being arrogant after achieving success, Laozi argued that the people shall try to avoid excessiveness, know how to be content, restrain their sharpness, maintain humility, and retreat at the right time. It emphasizes the importance of following the natural law of Dao with an aim to guide people to live and deal with things in a wiser, more peaceful, and nature-conforming way.

本章启示

做事要适度知足，追求事物不过盈，适时停下，且锋芒不可过露，学会内敛以长久保全自己。对待财富地位，应明白财富难守，富贵莫骄，否则自招灾祸。事业成功后，要遵循功成身退的智慧，顺应自然规律，避免贪恋权位名利而陷入危机。

The enlightenment of the chapter

When doing things, one should be moderately content. Avoid over-pursuing things, stop in a timely manner, and do not show off one's edge too much. Learn to be reserved in order to preserve oneself in the long run. Regarding wealth and status, one should understand that wealth is difficult to hold onto, and should not be arrogant when being wealthy or powerful, otherwise, it will bring disasters upon oneself. After achieving success in one's career, one should follow the wisdom of retreating after accomplishment, conform to the laws of nature, and avoid being mired in crises due to greed for power, position, fame, and wealth.

第十章

zài yíng pò bào yī néng wú lí hū tuán qì zhì róu néng yīng ér hū
载营魄抱一，能无离乎？抟[①]气致柔，能婴儿乎？
dí chú xuán jiàn néng wú cī hū tiān mén kāi hé néng wéi cí hū míng
涤除玄鉴[②]，能无疵乎？天门开阖，能为雌[③]乎？明
bái sì dá néng wú zhī hū ài mín zhì guó néng wú wéi hū
白四达，能无知乎？爱民治国，能无为乎？[④]

注释

① 抟：意为“凝聚”。通行本作“专”，通“抟”，义理一致，均强调精气的聚合。此处采用帛书本的表述。

② 玄鉴：“鉴”为“镜”，隐喻心境的明澈。通行本作“玄览”，“览”为观览，弱化了“镜喻”的认知论意义。此处采用帛书本，更贴合老子“涤除”（清除心垢）的意象系统。

③ 为雌：通行本作“无雌”，为讹误。此处采用帛书本的表述，符合老子“知雄守雌”（第二十八章）的核心主张。

④ 通行本“爱民治国，能无为乎？”原在“能无疵乎”后面，此处移至章末，更符合本章文意和逻辑顺序。安伦等认为前面五句有可能是老子冥修悟道的诀窍和要旨。通行本在本章末还有“生之畜之。生而不有，为而不恃，长而不宰，是谓玄德”一段，但与本章文意和逻辑不相关联，与第五十一章重复，疑是错简重出，据此删除。

今译

魂魄合一，能不分离吗？调气息致柔和，能像婴儿那样吗？静心内

观（洗涤玄奥的心境），能没有杂念吗？天地动静（感官与外界接触），能保持柔静吗？通晓四方，能没有心机（旁若无知）吗？爱民治国，能自然无为吗？

英译

In unifying your body and soul, can you avoid separation? In adjusting your breath to achieve softness, can you be like a baby? In cleansing the mystic mirror of your mind, can you be free from your mental distraction? In opening and closing your gate to Heaven, can you keep your inner peace? In perceiving all things, can you be free from cleverness? In loving the people and governing the state, can you keep to the principle of "wu-wei" (non-action)?

本章主旨

本章主要阐述了通过冥修中的调身、调息、调心等方法，实现身心合一，致虚守静，洞察世界真相，体悟"道"的奥秘，从而达到治理天下自然无为的理想状态。

The gist of the chapter

In this chapter, through the methods such as adjusting the body, regulating the breath, and calming the mind during meditation, one can achieve the unity and harmony of body and mind, attain mental void and keep to stillness, gain insight into the truth of the world, and understand the mystery of Dao, so as to achieve the ideal state of governing the state by following the principle of naturalness and "wu-wei" (non-action).

本章启示

修身要追求身心合一、专注纯粹，常净化心灵，清除杂念。治国理政及处世，应无为而治，不过度干预，顺势而为；保持守柔处下、内敛低调的态度；秉持无私奉献精神，有成绩而不居功自傲，如此方能提升修养、实现良好发展。

The enlightenment of the chapter

In cultivating one's moral character, one should pursue the unity of body and mind, focus with purity, constantly purify the soul, and eliminate distractions. In governing a state, handling affairs, and interacting with others, one should govern by "wu-wei" (non-action), not over-interfere, and act in accordance with the trend. One should maintain an attitude of being gentle, humble, and reserved, and keeping a low profile. One should uphold the spirit of selfless dedication. Even when achieving results, do not be conceited with one's achievements. Only in this way can one enhance his self-cultivation and attain sound development.

第十一章

sān shí fú gòng yī gǔ dāng qí wú yǒu chē zhī yòng shān zhí yǐ wéi
三十辐共一毂，当其无，有车之用。埏埴以为
qì dāng qí wú yǒu qì zhī yòng záo hù yǒu yǐ wéi shì dāng qí wú yǒu shì
器，当其无，有器之用。凿户牖以为室，当其无，有室
zhī yòng gù yǒu zhī yǐ wéi lì wú zhī yǐ wéi yòng
之用。故有之以为利，无之以为用。

今译

三十根辐条汇集到一个车毂当中，正因为车毂中间是空无的，才有了车的功用。糅合陶土制成器具，正因为器具中间是空无的，才有了器具的功用。开凿门窗建造房屋，正因为中间是空无的，才有了房屋的功用。所以，“有”给人以便利后，“无”才发挥其功用。

英译

Thirty spokes connect to one hub. It is just because of the empty space inside that the utility of the cart arises. Clay is molded into a vessel. It is just because of the empty space inside that the utility of the vessel arises. Doors and windows are cut out to make a house. It is just because of the empty space inside that the utility of the house arises. Therefore, being of things provides a condition; non-being of things functions as the utility.

本章主旨

本章通过列举车、器、室三个例子，形象地说明了“有”和“无”是相互依存、相互为用的关系。“有”指的是事物的实体部分，它们是具体存在的，能够为人们所直接感知和利用，给人带来便利；而“无”则是指事物中的虚空部分，这些看似无形的部分却恰恰是事物发挥其特定功能的关键所在。

The gist of the chapter

This chapter vividly illustrates through the examples of the cart, the vessel, and the house that “being” and “non-being” are interdependent and complementary. “Being” refers to the tangible parts of things which are concrete existences, and can be directly perceived and bring conveniences, while “non-being” refers to the empty or intangible parts of things. These seemingly intangible parts are precisely the key to the specific functions of things.

本章启示

一要重视无形要素，不仅仅关注有形实体，无形部分常具关键价值；二应辩证看待“有”“无”，平衡物质与精神追求，二者相互依存；三要懂得留白，无论是生活、工作还是人际交往，留有适当空间有利于发展。在现实生活中，人们往往更关注物质的拥有和积累等有形的方面，但实际上，很多时候无形的因素如空间、时间、情感、思想等，虽然看不见、摸不着，却对事物的发展和人们的生活有着深远的影响。

The enlightenment of the chapter

Firstly, we should attach importance to intangible elements and not merely focus on tangible entities. The intangible parts often possess crucial values. Secondly, we should view "being" and "non-being" dialectically, balance the pursuit of material and spiritual aspects, as the two are interdependent. Thirdly, we should understand the art of leaving blank spaces. Whether in life, work, or interpersonal relationships, appropriate space is conducive to development. In real life, people often pay more attention to the tangible aspects like material possessions and accumulations. In fact, many intangible factors such as space, time, emotions, and ideas, although invisible and intangible, have a profound impact on the development of things and the people's lives.

第十二章

wǔ sè lìng rén mù máng wǔ yīn lìng rén ěr lóng wǔ wèi lìng rén kǒu
五色令人目盲，五音令人耳聋，五味令人口
shuǎng chí chěng tián liè lìng rén xīn kuáng nán dé zhī huò lìng rén
爽；驰骋畋猎，令人心狂[1]；难得之货，令人
xíng fáng
行妨。

shì yǐ shèng rén wèi fù bù wèi mù
是以圣人为腹不为目。[2]

注释

① 心狂：通行本作“心发狂”，高亨认为“发”是衍字，“心狂”其义已足，且“驰骋畋猎，令人心狂；难得之货，令人行妨”句法一律，符合老子修辞和简练文风。据此予以调整。

② 通行本本章及第三十八章、第七十三章的末尾还有“故去彼取此”一句，高亨等认为是后人添加，与前文“是以”句子的意思有重复之嫌，语义、修辞累赘，不符合老子简练风格，据此删除。

今译

五色使人眼花缭乱，五音使人听觉不敏，五味使人味觉受损；纵情狩猎使人心发狂，稀罕货物使人行为不轨。

所以，圣人但求温饱，不为纵情声色之娱。

英译

The five colors may blind eyes, the five tones may deafen ears, the five flavors may dull tastes, horse-racing and hunting may madden the mind, and rare goods may cause bad behaviors.

Therefore, the sage provides for the stomach, not for the eyes.

本章主旨

本章提醒人们过度追求外在物质享受的危害，倡导要学会审视自己的生活方式，不要过度沉迷于物质追求，而是要回归内心，追求内在的充实与满足，遵循简朴、自然的生活方式。

The gist of the chapter

This chapter warns people to be vigilant against the harm of excessive material pursuits and sensory pleasures, and advocates that we should learn to examine our own way of life, avoid excessive indulgence in material pursuits, and seek the inner enrichment and contentment, following a simple and natural way of life.

本章启示

须警惕感官诱惑，避免因过度沉溺而迷失自我、损害身心；要注重内在精神需求，而非盲目追逐物质享受，应以提升修养充实内心；还应坚守自我，不随波逐流，依据自身价值观做出选择。

The enlightenment of the chapter

One should be vigilant against sensory temptations to avoid losing oneself and harming the body and mind due to excessive indulgence.

We should focus on inner spiritual needs rather than blindly pursuing material enjoyment. We should enhance our self-cultivation to enrich ourselves. Moreover, we should adhere to our true selves, not follow the crowd blindly, and make choices based on our own values.

第十三章

chǒng rǔ ruò jīng guì dà huàn ruò shēn
宠辱若惊，贵大患若身。

hé wéi chǒng rǔ ruò jīng chǒng wéi xià dé zhī ruò jīng shī zhī ruò jīng shì wèi chǒng rǔ ruò jīng
何为宠辱若惊？宠为下，得之若惊，失之若惊，是谓宠辱若惊。

hé wèi guì dà huàn ruò shēn wú suǒ yǐ yǒu dà huàn zhě wèi wú yǒu shēn jí wú wú shēn wú yǒu hé huàn
何谓贵大患若身？吾所以有大患者，为吾有身；及吾无身，吾有何患？

gù guì yǐ shēn wéi tiān xià ruò kě jì tiān xià ài yǐ shēn wéi tiān xià ruò kě tuō tiān xià
故贵以身为天下，若可寄天下；爱以身为天下，若可托天下。

今译

得宠和受辱都使人惊慌，重视祸患就像重视自己的身体。

什么叫得宠和受辱都使人惊慌？因为受宠是卑下的，得宠了会感到惊慌，失宠了也会感到惊慌，这就叫作得宠和受辱都使人惊慌。

什么叫重视祸患就像重视自己的身体？我之所以有祸患，是因为我有这个身体，如果我没有这个身体，我还有什么祸患呢？

因此，只有像珍视自己的身体那样珍视天下，才可以把天下寄托给他；只有像爱惜自己的身体那样爱惜天下，才可以把天下托付给他。

英译

Being favored and being disgraced may both disturb one's mind, and calamity is regarded as critical as oneself.

What is meant by "Being favored and being disgraced may both disturb one's mind"? Being favored means a low position. Thus, receiving it disturbs one's mind; losing it disturbs one's mind. Such is called "Being favored and being disgraced may both disturb one's mind".

What is meant by "Calamity is regarded as critical as oneself"? The reason why I have calamity is that I have a self. Once I had no self, what calamity could I have?

Therefore, if one values the world as his self, the world can be entrusted with his governance; if one loves the world as his self, the world can be entrusted to his care.

本章主旨

本章老子认为人们对于宠辱的态度往往是"宠辱若惊"，即无论是得宠还是受辱都会感到惊恐不安。这是因为人们过于在意身外之物，对外部认可过度依赖，失去了内心的平静。同样，人们之所以会有大患，是因为过分执着于自身的存在和利益，只有超越这种对"自身"的执着，才能真正摆脱祸患的困扰。老子认为，理想的统治者不会只关注自己的私利，而是将天下的利益放在首位，像关心自己的身体一样关心天下百姓的疾苦，像爱护自己的生命一样爱护天下万物。

The gist of the chapter

In this chapter, Laozi believes that being favored and being disgraced may both disturb one's mind. It is because people are too concerned about external things and over-dependent on external recognition, they lose their inner peace. Similarly, the reason why people have calamities is that they are too attached to their own existence and interests. Only by transcending this attachment to "self" can they truly get rid of the troubles of calamities. Laozi advocates that the ideal ruler shall not only focus on his own interest, but put the interests of the world first, care about the suffering of the people in the world as much as his self, and love all things in the world as much as his self.

本章启示

一是正确看待宠辱，不被外界评价左右，保持平和心态，避免患得患失；二是重视自身，不过分计较个人得失，树立将个人与天下相联系的价值观；三是提升责任感，以担当天下的胸怀，在生活和工作中积极尽责，实现更大价值。

The enlightenment of the chapter

Firstly, we should have a correct attitude towards favor and disgrace, not be swayed by external evaluations, maintain a peaceful mindset, and avoid being overly concerned about gains and losses. Secondly, we should attach importance to ourselves, not overly haggle over personal gains and losses, and establish a value system that links the individual to the world. Thirdly, we should enhance our sense of responsibility, with the broad-mindedness to take on the responsibility of the world, actively fulfill our duties in life and work, and achieve greater value.

第十四章

shì zhī bù jiàn míng yuē yí tīng zhī bù wén míng yuē xī bó zhī bù dé
视之不见，名曰夷；听之不闻，名曰希；搏之不得，
míng yuē wēi cǐ sān zhě bù kě zhì jié gù hùn ér wéi yī qí shàng bù jiǎo
名曰微。此三者不可致诘，故混而为一。其上不皦，
qí xià bù mèi mǐn mǐn bù kě míng fù guī yú wú wù shì wèi wú zhuàng zhī
其下不昧，绳绳不可名，复归于无物。是谓无状之
zhuàng wú wù zhī xiàng shì wèi hū huǎng yíng zhī bù jiàn qí shǒu suí zhī bù
状，无物之象，是谓惚恍。迎之不见其首，随之不
jiàn qí hòu
见其后。

zhí gǔ zhī dào yǐ yù jīn zhī yǒu néng zhī gǔ shǐ shì wèi dào jì
执古之道，以御今之有。能知古始，是谓道纪。

今译

看它看不见，叫作“夷”；听它听不到，叫作“希”；摸它摸不着，叫作“微”。这三者无法探究把握，它是浑然一体的。它上面不显得明亮，下面也不显得昏暗，绵绵不断而不可名状，又回归到无形无物的状态。这就叫作没有形状的形状、没有物体的形象，可称其为“惚恍”。迎着它，看不见它的前头；随着它，又看不见它的后面。

把握古来的道，来驾驭现在的具体事物。能够认识宇宙的起始，可以说是道的纲纪。

英译

Being looked at, yet it cannot be seen. So we call it the Invisible.

Being listened to, yet it cannot be heard. So we call it the Inaudible. Being reached for, yet it cannot be touched. So we call it the Intangible. These three cannot be fathomed, and are thus blended into one. Its upper part is not bright, and its lower part is not dim. Ceaseless, it cannot be named, and reverts again to the state of nothingness. It is called the form of formlessness and the image of nothingness. Hence it is called the Elusive. Meeting it, we cannot see its front; following it, we cannot see its back.

By holding to the ancient Dao, we can govern things at present. Being able to know the primeval beginning of the universe is called the law of Dao.

本章主旨

本章主要对“道”的属性进行描述。“道”是超越人类视觉、听觉、触觉等感官认知的存在。“道”具有超越性、永恒性和无限性，是无始无终、无边无际的，超越了时间和空间的限制，是永恒不变的存在。“道”具有神秘性，是宇宙万物运行和发展的根本动力和源泉。老子认为，要把握自古以来就存在的“道”，以此来驾驭和理解当下的具体事物。了解宇宙的初始，认识“道”的规律，是把握“道”的关键所在。

The gist of the chapter

This chapter mainly describes the attributes of Dao. Dao is an existence that transcends human sensory perceptions such as sight, hearing, and touch. Dao has the attributes of transcendence, eternity, and infinity. Dao is without beginning or end. It is boundless and limitless. It transcends the limitations of time and space and is an eternal and unchanging existence. Dao contains infinite mysteries, and is the fundamental driving force and source for the operation and development of all things in the universe. Laozi believes that grasping the ancient Dao can harness and understand the specific things at present. Being able to understand the primeval beginning of the universe and understanding the law of Dao is the key to grasping Dao.

本章启示

突破感官局限，不能仅靠直观感受认知世界，要运用理性思维深化认知；透过表象把握事物本质，“道”虽无形却统摄万物，须深入探究规律；以史为鉴，汲取传统智慧，遵循古老的“道”来应对当下事务。

The enlightenment of the chapter

To break through the limitations of the human senses, one cannot rely solely on intuitive feelings to understand the world. Instead, rational thinking should be employed to deepen cognition. Grasp the essence of things through appearances. Although Dao is intangible, it governs all things, so we need to delve into the laws. Take history as a mirror, draw on traditional wisdom, and follow the ancient Dao to handle current affairs.

第十五章

gǔ zhī shàn wéi dào zhě　wēi miào xuán tōng　shēn bù kě shí
古之善为道者[①]，微妙玄通，深不可识。

fú wéi bù kě shí　gù qiáng wéi zhī róng　yù xī ruò dōng shè chuān　yóu xī ruò wèi sì lín　yǎn xī qí ruò kè　huàn xī qí ruò shì　dàn xī qí ruò hǎi　liù xī ruò wú zhǐ　dūn xī qí ruò pǔ　kuàng xī qí ruò gǔ　hùn xī qí ruò zhuó
夫唯不可识，故强为之容：豫兮若冬涉川，犹兮若畏四邻，俨兮其若客，涣兮其若释，澹兮其若海，飂兮若无止[②]，敦兮其若朴，旷兮其若谷，混兮其若浊。

shú néng zhuó yǐ jìng zhī xú qīng　shú néng ān yǐ dòng zhī xú shēng　bǎo cǐ dào zhě bù yù yíng　fú wéi bù yíng　gù néng bì ér xīn chéng
孰能浊以静之徐清？孰能安以动之徐生？保此道者不欲盈。夫唯不盈，故能蔽而新成[③]。

注释

① 善为道者：王弼本作“善为士者”。“道者”更直接指向修道之人，强化了与“道”的关联，更具超然性，故据帛书乙本、傅奕本等校正。

② 通行本“澹兮其若海，飂兮若无止”原在第二十章的相关段落，但与该章上下文语义、逻辑不相关联，句式也不同，疑是错简。据安伦等校勘，调整至本章。

③ 蔽而新成：王弼本作“蔽不新成”。据高亨等考证，“而”“不”篆文形近，“不”系“而”之误字。“蔽而新成”与“蔽则新”（第二十二章）一致，符合老子本意，据此校正。

今译

古代善于行道的人，精妙入微，通达玄奥，如此精深，（常人）难以认识。正因为难以认识，所以只能勉强来形容他们：小心谨慎啊，像冬天踏冰过河；犹豫警觉啊，像提防四周邻居；庄重严肃啊，像尊贵的客人；温暖可亲啊，像冰凌消融；淡泊恬静啊，像深沉的大海；自由飘逸啊，像不知停止的疾风；敦厚质朴啊，像未经雕琢的木材；空旷豁达啊，像幽深的山谷；浑朴醇厚啊，像一汪浊水。

谁能让浊水静下来慢慢澄清？谁能让事物安定后慢慢生长？持守此道的人不求盈满。正因为不求盈满，所以能够去旧更新。

英译

Those ancients who practiced Dao well were subtle, mysterious, and insightful. They were so profound that they could not be understood. As they were beyond our knowledge, I could only attempt to describe them as follows: Cautious, like one crossing a frozen stream in winter. Alert, like one fearing the danger all around. Solemn, like a distinguished guest. Softening, like melting ice. Detached, like the vast sea. Unrestrained, like the ceaseless wind. Natural, like uncarved wood. Inclusive, like a deep valley. Mixed, like muddy water.

Who can make the muddy water still, and let it gradually become clear? Who can stabilize things, and move them into gradual growth? Those who keep to Dao do not seek to be overfull. It is just because they do not seek to be overfull that they can accomplish renewal after turning old.

本章主旨

本章主要描述了善为道者的谨慎、警惕、端庄、温和、恬静、超然、淳朴、豁达、包容等行为表现和品质。正因为他们对“道”有着深刻的理解和体悟，才有这样高深的境界和精神气质。在此基础上阐述了动静之道、不盈之道的智慧。在面对纷繁复杂、混乱不清的局面或内心的杂念时，应保持内心的平静与安宁；在安稳平静的状态下，要适时地采取行动，让生命和事物焕发出新的生机与活力。不追求过度的满足和盈满，能够在旧的事物中不断地推陈出新，实现自我的超越和持续的发展，体现了一种顺应自然、遵循“道”的规律的智慧和境界。

The gist of the chapter

This chapter mainly describes the specific behavior and qualities of those ancient masters in Dao such as being cautious, vigilant, dignified, gentle, detached, unrestrained, natural, inclusive, tolerant, etc. It is just because they have a deep understanding of Dao that they have such a profound realm and spiritual temperament. In addition, Laozi expounded the wisdom of movement and stillness, and seeking no fullness. In the face of the complicated and chaotic situations or mental distractions, one should maintain inner peace and tranquility; while in the state of stability, one should take timely actions to bring about new vitality and gradual growth. Without seeking excessive satisfaction and fullness, we can constantly accomplish renewal after turning old, to achieve self-transcendence and sustainable development, which reflects the wisdom of conforming to natural and constant law of Dao.

本章启示

行事要谨慎，对周围事物保持敬畏；注重修养身心，培养质朴、豁达与包容的内在品质；懂得动静结合，混乱中宁静以求解，安稳时主动求变；秉持谦逊态度，不骄傲自满，如此方能不断进取、实现自我更新。

The enlightenment of the chapter

Be cautious in your actions and maintain a sense of awe towards the things around you. Pay attention to cultivating your body and mind, fostering inner qualities such as simplicity, open-mindedness, and tolerance. Understand the combination of action and stillness. Seek solutions in tranquility amidst chaos and take the initiative to change in times of stability. Adopt a humble attitude, avoid being arrogant and complacent, and only then can you keep making progress and achieve self-perfection.

第十六章

zhì xū jí shǒu jìng dǔ
致虚极，守静笃。

wàn wù bìng zuò wú yǐ guān fù fú wù yún yún gè fù guī qí gēn guī
万物并作，吾以观复。夫物芸芸，各复归其根。归
gēn yuē jìng jìng yuē fù mìng fù mìng yuē cháng zhī cháng yuē míng bù zhī
根曰静，静曰复命，复命曰常，知常曰明。不知
cháng wàng zuò xiōng
常，妄作，凶。

zhī cháng róng róng nǎi gōng gōng nǎi quán quán nǎi tiān tiān nǎi dào
知常容，容乃公，公乃全①，全乃天，天乃道，
dào nǎi jiǔ mò shēn bù dài
道乃久，没身不殆。

注释

① 全：通行本作“王”，据陈鼓应等考证，“王”字是“全”字缺损所误，故将其改正。

今译

达到极致虚空，守住极度清静。

万物生长变化，我从中观察它们的循环往复。世间万物纷繁众多，各自回归到它们的根本。回归根本就叫作虚静，虚静就是复归生命的本真。复归生命本真就叫作恒常规律，认识恒常规律就叫作明智。如果不认识恒常规律而妄自作为，就会有凶险。

认识恒常规律就能包容，包容就能公正，公正才能周全，周全才符合自然，符合自然才符合大道，符合大道才能长久，终身才没有危险。

英译

Attain ultimate void; keep extreme stillness. All things arise and grow, I watch them return. All things will return to their roots. Returning to their roots is called stillness; stillness is called returning to their destiny. Returning to their destiny is called the eternal law; knowing the eternal law is called enlightenment. Not knowing the eternal law, yet acting rashly, leads to trouble.

Knowing the eternal law can be inclusive; inclusiveness can be impartial; impartiality can be thoroughness; thoroughness conforms to nature; nature conforms to Dao; Dao leads to longevity, and one will avoid danger throughout life.

本章主旨

本章强调了致虚守静的重要性，认为通过保持心灵的虚空和清静，可以更好地观察和领悟万物的规律，即“道”。在面对生活和工作中的各种问题时，要遵循事物发展的规律，不盲目冲动，不妄自作为，只有这样才能避免不必要的风险和挫折，才能懂得包容和理解他人，不固执己见，不以偏见待人，做到公正公平，建立良好的人际关系，促进社会的和谐发展。

The gist of the chapter

This chapter emphasizes the importance of attaining void and keeping stillness, and believes that by maintaining void and stillness, one can better observe and understand the laws of all things, i. e., “Dao”. When facing various problems in life and work, we must follow the laws of the development of things, without being blindly impulsive and acting rashly. Only in this way can we avoid unnecessary risks and setbacks, know how to tolerate and understand others, not stubborn, not biased towards others, and achieve fairness. Only in this way can we establish good interpersonal relationships and promote the harmonious development of society.

本章启示

一要追求内心宁静，在喧嚣中排除干扰，洞察事物本质；二要遵循事物规律，顺势而为，避免盲目行动导致不良后果；三要培养包容豁达胸怀，秉持公正态度，周全行事，实现与自然、社会和谐共生及长久发展。

The enlightenment of the chapter

Firstly, pursue inner peace. Filter out distractions amidst the hustle and bustle and perceive the essence of things. Secondly, abide by the laws of things, act in accordance with the trend, and avoid adverse consequences caused by blind actions. Thirdly, cultivate an inclusive and open-minded attitude, uphold justice, act in a comprehensive manner, and achieve harmonious co-existence and long-term development with nature and society.

第十七章

tài shàng　xià zhī yǒu zhī　qí cì　qīn ér yù zhī　qí cì　wèi zhī　qí cì
太上，下知有之。其次，亲而誉之。其次，畏之。其次，
wǔ zhī
侮之。

xìn bù zú yān　yǒu bù xìn yān　yóu xī　qí guì yán　gōng chéng shì suì　bǎi
信不足焉，有不信焉。犹兮其贵言。功成事遂，百
xìng jiē wèi wǒ zì rán
姓皆谓我自然①。

注释

① 自然：老子所说的“自然”不是现代意义上的自然界，而是指事物自然而然、本来如此、本性使然的状态，即事物自然而然的存在和发展方式，没有外在的强制干预、强作妄为和强制力量。

今译

最好的统治者，人们只知道有他的存在。其次一等，人们亲近和赞美他。再次一等，人们畏惧他。最次一等，人们轻侮他。

统治者诚信不足，人们就会不信任他。统治者应谨慎行事而不随意发号施令。功业成就，事情顺遂，百姓都说：“我们本来就是这样啊。”

英译

The best rulers are merely known of their existence. The next best are loved and praised. The next are feared. The worst are reviled. If the rulers lack faith, the people will not trust them. The rulers shall be prudent, and be careful in what they say. When their missions are accomplished and their work done, the people would all remark: "We are naturally like this."

本章主旨

本章老子通过对统治者不同治理境界的描述，强调了无为而治的重要性和统治者诚信的意义。老子认为，统治者应该顺应自然规律，减少对百姓生活的干预，以达到"功成事遂，百姓皆谓我自然"的理想状态。

The gist of the chapter

Laozi in this chapter, through the description of the rulers' different governance realms, emphasizes the importance of governance with non-contrived actions and the significance of the rulers' trustworthiness. Laozi believes that the ruler should conform to the laws of nature and reduce the interference in the lives of the people, so as to achieve the ideal state of "when missions are accomplished and things are going well, the people would remark that this is how they are naturally are".

本章启示

领导者应追求"润物细无声"的管理境界，构建良好体系让组织自行运转；注重诚信，以言行一致赢得信任；谨言慎行，靠实际行动引领示范；尊重个体，激发自主性，让成员在实现目标中感受自我价值。

The enlightenment of the chapter

Leaders should pursue the management realm of "nourishing things like spring rain, softly and silently", constructing a sound system to enable the organization to operate on its own. They should attach importance to integrity and win trust by matching words with their deeds. Be cautious in words and actions, leading by practical examples. Respect individuals, stimulate their initiatives, and enable members to feel their self-worth while achieving goals.

第十八章

dà dào fèi ān yǒu rén yì liù qīn bù hé ān yǒu xiào cí guó jiā hūn
大道废，安有仁义？六亲不和，安有孝慈？国家昏
luàn ān yǒu zhèng chén
乱，安有正臣？①

注释

① 本章采用竹简本的文句。通行本作“大道废，有仁义；智慧出，有大伪；六亲不和，有孝慈；国家昏乱，有正臣”。而“智慧出，有大伪”，疑是战国中后期受到庄子后学中激烈派思想影响衍生出来的表述。正臣：通行本作“忠臣”，帛书本作“贞臣”，竹简本作“正臣”，“正”与“贞”古代通用，故据竹简本、帛书本校正。

今译

大道废弃了，哪还有仁义？六亲不和了，哪还有孝慈？国家混乱了，哪还有忠臣？

英译

When the Great Dao is abandoned, how can there still be benevolence and righteousness? When the six kinship relatives are not in harmony, how can there still be filial piety? When the country is in chaos, how can there still be loyal ministers?

本章主旨

本章老子揭示了背离大道、六亲不和及国家混乱所导致的道德沦丧、虚伪、不忠等后果和弊端，从另一个侧面倡导人们应回归自然之道，遵循大道。

The gist of the chapter

In this chapter, Laozi reveals the consequences and drawbacks of moral decay, hypocrisy, and disloyalty caused by deviation from the Great Dao, discord between the six kinship relatives, and the state chaos. From another perspective, he advocates that people should return to the way of nature and follow the Great Dao.

本章启示

要回归事物本质，追求大道。在社会与道德方面，道德与社会环境相关，要警惕其形式化；在家庭关系上，和谐是孝慈的基础，成员应相互理解包容；在国家治理与人才层面，治理者要营造清明环境，人才与环境相互依存。

The enlightenment of the chapter

We should return to the essence of things and pursue the Great Dao. In terms of society and morality, morality is related to the social environment, and we should be vigilant against ritualization. Regarding family relations, harmony is the foundation of filial piety and kindness, and family members should understand and tolerate each other. In terms of national governance and talents, governors should create a clean and just environment, and talents and the environment are interdependent.

第十九章

jué zhì qì biàn mín lì bǎi bèi jué wěi qì zhà mín fù xiào cí jué qiǎo qì lì dào zéi wú yǒu

绝智弃辩，民利百倍。绝伪弃诈，民复孝慈。绝巧弃利，盗贼无有。[1]

cǐ sān yán yǐ wéi wén bù zú gù lìng yǒu suǒ shǔ jiàn sù bào pǔ shǎo sī guǎ yù jué xué wú yōu

此三言以为文不足，故令有所属：见素抱朴，少私寡欲，绝学无忧[2]。

注释

① 本章采用竹简本“绝智弃辩”“绝伪弃诈”的文句，通行本作“绝圣弃智”“绝仁弃义”，疑是战国中后期受到庄子后学中激烈派思想影响对儒家伦理（仁义）的批判，反映战国末期至汉初的思想冲突激化。

② 通行本“绝学无忧”原在第二十章句首，但语义与该章内容不相关联，疑是错简，故调整至本章。

今译

摒弃巧辩，人们可以获利百倍。摒弃伪诈，人们可以恢复孝慈。摒弃诈利，盗贼才不会出现。

（智辩、伪诈、巧利）这三方面都是巧饰，不足以治理天下，所以要使人们行为有所归属：保持纯真和质朴，减少私心和欲望，摒弃巧饰之学而避免忧患。

英译

Abandoning cleverness and discarding arguments, people can profit a hundredfold. Abandoning hypocrisy and discarding contrivance, people can restore filial piety. Abandoning tricks and discarding personal interests, thieves and robbers will not appear.

These three aspects are still not enough to govern the world, so people's behavior needs to be made to the following: maintain innocence and simplicity, reduce selfishness and desires, and renounce the learning (of tricks) to avoid troubles.

本章主旨

本章老子认为智辩、伪诈、巧利的观念会扭曲自然的社会秩序和人们的本性，应该被杜绝和摒弃。他倡导人们回归自然、纯真的本性，这样才能实现社会的和谐与安定。

The gist of the chapter

In this chapter, Laozi believes that cleverness and arguments, hypocrisy and contrivance, tricks and fraudulence will distort the natural social order and people's nature, and should be eliminated and rejected. He advocates that people shall return to their nature of simplicity and innocence, so as to achieve social harmony and stability.

本章启示

在社会治理层面，启示治理者应摒弃机巧权谋、追求功利及虚伪欺诈的治理方式，以营造安定、诚信的社会环境，让百姓回归孝慈；在个人修养层面，倡导人们保持朴素纯真，减少私欲，从而获得内心平静，提升精神境界。

The enlightenment of the chapter

On the level of social governance, it serves as an inspiration for governors to eschew governance methods marked by devious stratagems, the unbridled pursuit of self-serving interests, and the prevalence of hypocrisy and fraud. By doing so, they can foster a stable and trustworthy social milieu where the populace can revert to the noble virtues of filial piety and parental affection. In terms of personal cultivation, it exhorts individuals to uphold simplicity and purity, curtail their selfish desires. This way, they can attain inner tranquility and ascend to a higher spiritual plane.

第二十章

wéi zhī yǔ hē xiāng qù jǐ hé měi zhī yǔ ě xiāng qù hé ruò rén zhī
唯之与呵[①]，相去几何？美之与恶，相去何若？人之
suǒ wèi bù kě bù wèi huāng xī qí wèi yāng zāi
所畏，不可不畏。荒兮，其未央哉！

zhòng rén xī xī rú xiǎng tài láo rú chūn dēng tái wǒ dú bó xī qí
众人熙熙，如享太牢，如春登台。我独泊兮，其
wèi zhào dùn dùn xī rú yīng ér zhī wèi hái léi léi xī ruò wú suǒ guī
未兆；沌沌兮，如婴儿之未孩；儽儽兮，若无所归。
zhòng rén jiē yǒu yú ér wǒ dú ruò yí wǒ yú rén zhī xīn yě zāi
众人皆有余，而我独若遗。我愚人之心也哉。

sú rén zhāo zhāo wǒ dú hūn hūn sú rén chá chá wǒ dú mèn mèn
俗人昭昭，我独昏昏；俗人察察，我独闷闷。[②]
zhòng rén jiē yǒu yǐ ér wǒ dú wán qiě bǐ wǒ dú yì yú rén ér guì
众人皆有以，而我独顽且鄙。我独异于人，而贵
shí mǔ
食母。

注释

① 通行本本章句首原有“绝学无忧”文句，但其语义与本章内容不相关联，疑是错简，故调整至第十九章。唯之与呵：通行本作“唯之与阿”。“呵”表示大声呵斥，此处采用竹简本和帛书本的表述。

② 通行本在“我独闷闷”后还有“澹兮其若海，飂兮若无止”一句，但与上下文句式不同，语义不相关联。据安伦等校勘，调整至第十五章的相应位置。

今译

唯诺与呵斥，相差有多大？美善与丑恶，差别又大多？人们所畏惧的，不能不畏惧。天荒地老（广漠无边），好像没有尽头。

众人兴高采烈，好像参加丰盛的筵席，好像春天登上高台远眺。唯独我淡泊恬静，无动于衷，混混沌沌，像不会嬉笑的婴儿；漂泊无依，好像无家可归。众人都丰足有余，唯独我有所不足。我真是愚人的心啊！

世人都明明白白，唯独我糊里糊涂；世人都精明机灵，唯独我懵懂无知。众人都有本领，唯独我愚顽笨拙。我独与众不同，只尊崇养育万物的母亲（“道”）。

英译

How much difference is there between yes and no? How much difference is there between good and evil? What the people fear cannot also be feared. How vast it is, as if there is no end.

All the others are bustling with delight, as though feasting on a sacred banquet or ascending a terrace in springtime. Yet I alone remain still and detached, untouched by such revelry. Simple and unknowing, I am like an infant yet to utter a smile. Adrift and weary, I have no haven to call my own. All the others abound in excess, while I alone seem bereft. Am I truly the fool at heart?

The multitudes are clear-headed, while I alone am muddle-headed. They are so shrewd, while I alone am dull. They are capable, while I alone am stubborn and clumsy. I differ from others in that I alone revere the Mother of all things—Dao.

本章主旨

本章老子通过对自己与众人在行为、心境、价值追求等方面差异的对比，表达了对世俗的批判和对“道”的追求。他认为世人过于追求名利和享受，被各种表象迷惑，而自己则追求一种淡泊、纯真、自由的精神境界及尊道守道的原则。

The gist of the chapter

In this chapter, Laozi expresses his criticism of the secular world and his pursuit of Dao by comparing the differences between himself and others in behavior, state of mind and value pursuit. He believes that the world pursues fame, wealth and enjoyment too much, and is deceived by various appearances, while he pursues a simple, natural and free spiritual realm and the principle of respecting and following Dao.

本章启示

一是保持独立思考，不盲目跟从世俗潮流，依据自身价值观做选择；二是坚守内心本真，不为虚荣功利所动，守护质朴纯净的内心；三是以平和心态看待得失，不被一时境遇或与他人差距影响；四是追求精神富足，重视内在滋养，关注精神世界提升。

The enlightenment of the chapter

Firstly, foster and maintain independent thinking. Resist the temptation to blindly trail the secular tides. Instead, base your decisions on your own deeply-held values, firmly rooted in your personal belief system. Secondly, remain steadfast in upholding your inner authenticity. Do not allow yourself to be lured astray by the allure of vanity and the cold-heartedness of utilitarianism. Protect and cherish your simple and untainted heart, for it is the wellspring of your true self. Thirdly, approach gains and losses with a peaceful mindset. Refrain from being swayed by transient circumstances or the disparities you perceive between yourself and others. Remember that true worth is not measured by momentary achievements or comparisons. Fourthly, earnestly pursue spiritual richness. Place great emphasis on the nourishment of your inner self, devoting time and energy to self-reflection and growth. Pay close attention to the continuous elevation of your spiritual realm, for it is in this domain that true fulfillment lies.

第二十一章

kǒng dé zhī róng wéi dào shì cóng dào zhī wéi wù wéi huǎng wéi hū hū
孔德之容，惟道是从。道之为物，惟恍惟惚。惚
xī huǎng xī qí zhōng yǒu xiàng huǎng xī hū xī qí zhōng yǒu wù yǎo xī
兮恍兮，其中有象；恍兮惚兮，其中有物；窈兮
míng xī qí zhōng yǒu jīng qí jīng shèn zhēn qí zhōng yǒu xìn
冥兮，其中有精；其精甚真，其中有信。

zì jīn jí gǔ qí míng bù qù yǐ yuè zhòng fǔ wú hé yǐ zhī zhòng fǔ
自今及古[1]，其名不去，以阅众甫。吾何以知众甫
zhī rán zāi yǐ cǐ
之然[2]哉？以此。

注释

① 自今及古：通行本作“自古及今”，帛书本作“自今及古”。高亨等认为，“道”这个物古时就有，而“道”这个名是老子今时给的，故用“道”的名以称古时的物，应是“自今及古”。故据帛书本等校正。

② 众甫之然：王弼本作“众甫之状”。“然”表示原委和本原，与“状”有区别，帛书本、河上公本等作“然”，据此校正。

今译

大德的形态完全依从于道。道这个东西，总是恍恍惚惚的。恍恍惚惚啊，这当中又有迹象；恍恍惚惚啊，这当中又有物象。深远暗昧啊，这当中又有精质，这精质非常真实，这当中又是可信验的。

从当今上溯到古代，它的名字永远不会消失。根据它可以认识万物的本原，我凭什么认识万物的本原呢？就是凭借它（“道”）啊。

英译

The manifestations of great virtue is in complete accordance with Dao. Dao as a thing is elusive and intangible. Elusive and intangible! Yet within it are images. Intangible and elusive! Yet within it are entities. Profound and obscure! Yet within it is the essence. The essence is very real, and within it is something that can be verified.

From the present to ancient times, its name has never disappeared. By means of it, we can observe the origins of all things. How do I know the states of all things? By means of this.

本章主旨

这一章主要阐述了“道”的特质，以及“道”与“德”、“道”与“万物”的关系。一方面，细致描述了“道”的那种恍惚、幽深却又真实存在且蕴含规律的特性；另一方面，着重指出了“德”依从于“道”，以及“道”是认识万物根源和发展变化的关键所在。追寻、体悟那个看似无形却无处不在、作用非凡的“道”，按照“道”的指引去生活、去认识世间万物。

The gist of the chapter

This chapter mainly expounds the characteristics of Dao and the relationship between Dao and De, and Dao and all things. On the one hand, it describes in detail the trance, deep but real characteristics of Dao which contains laws; on the other hand, it emphasizes that De conforms to Dao, and Dao is the key to understanding the root and development of all things. By pursuing and comprehending the seemingly invisible but ubiquitous and extraordinary “Dao”, you can live and understand all things in the world according to the guidance of Dao.

本章启示

要认识到无形力量的存在，深入探索事物本质，不局限于表面；遵循自然与社会规律，顺势而为，达成目标；面对不确定性坚定信念，相信事物有内在本质与秩序；以宏观、长远视角看待事物，从历史与整体趋势把握发展走向。

The enlightenment of the chapter

One should recognize the existence of intangible forces, delve deep into the essence of things, and not be confined to the surface. Abide by the laws of nature and society, act in accordance with the trends to achieve goals. When faced with uncertainties, strengthen your conviction and believe that things have an inherent essence and order. Adopt a macroscopic and long-term vantage point to perceive things. Delve into historical and overarching trends to accurately discern and firmly grasp the development trajectory.

第二十二章

qū zé quán wǎng zé zhí wā zé yíng bì zé xīn shǎo zé duō duō zé huò
曲则全，枉则直，洼则盈，敝则新，少则多[①]，多则惑。

shì yǐ shèng rén bào yī wéi tiān xià shì bù zì xiàn gù míng bù zì shì gù zhāng bù zì fá gù yǒu gōng bù zì jīn gù zhǎng
是以圣人抱一为天下式，不自见，故明；不自是，故彰；不自伐，故有功；不自矜，故长。

fú wéi bù zhēng gù tiān xià mò néng yǔ zhī zhēng gǔ zhī suǒ wèi qū zé quán zhě qǐ xū yán zāi chéng quán ér guī zhī
夫唯不争，故天下莫能与之争。古之所谓"曲则全"者，岂虚言哉！诚全而归之。

注释

① 少则多：王弼本等作"少则得"，而帛书本等作"少则多"，符合每句用词的正反相对，据此校正。

今译

委屈反能保全，弯曲反能伸直，低洼反能充盈，敝旧反能更新，少取反能多得，多得反会迷惑。

所以，圣人持守道作为天下的范式。不自我表现，所以反能昭明；不自以为是，所以反能彰显；不自我夸耀，所以反能见功；不自骄自傲，所以反能长久。

正因为与人不争，所以天下没有人能与其相争。古人所说的“委屈反能保全”怎么会是虚假的话呢?！它实实在在能保全自己。

英译

Enduring grievances leads to self-preservation; being crooked results in straightening; being hollow allows for filling; being worn out makes way for renewal; having less brings more; having more causes confusion.

Therefore, the sage holds on to the One as the model for the world. By not showing off oneself, one becomes clear-sighted; by not being self-righteous, one becomes conspicuous; by not boasting about oneself, one achieves merit; by not being conceited, one attains growth.

Because of not contending with others, no one in the world can contend with him. Is what was said in ancient times about "Enduring grievances leads to self-preservation" just empty words? Truly, preservation comes to those who follow it.

本章主旨

本章主要阐述了圣人持守大道的处世哲学及一系列辩证关系。主张人们要学会以退为进、谦虚低调、不与人争，通过坚守“不争之道”的原则来实现个人的成长和发展。

The gist of the chapter

This chapter mainly expounds the sage's philosophy of life and a series of dialectical relationships. It advocates that people should learn to advance by retreating, be humble and low-key, and not compete with others, and achieve personal growth and development by adhering to the principle of non-contention.

本章启示

懂得以迂回、让步的方式行事，以退为进达成目标；保持谦逊，低调不张扬，客观认识自我与外界，赢得认可；学会舍弃，避免贪多，专注重要事物以获成就；秉持“不争”态度，专注自我成长，以和为贵，以实力脱颖而出。

The enlightenment of the chapter

Understand how to act in a circuitous and concessive manner, retreating in order to advance and achieve goals. Remain humble, keep a low profile, objectively understand oneself and the outside world, and win recognition. Learn to give up what is unnecessary, avoid being greedy for more, and focus on important matters to achieve success. Adopt an attitude of "non-contention", devote full attention to self-growth, attach great importance to harmony, and distinguish oneself through sheer strength.

第二十三章

xī yán zì rán gù piāo fēng bù zhōng zhāo zhòu yǔ bù zhōng rì shú wèi
希言自然。故飘风不终朝，骤雨不终日。孰为
cǐ zhě tiān dì tiān dì shàng bù néng jiǔ ér kuàng yú rén hū
此者？天地。天地尚不能久，而况于人乎？

gù cóng shì yú dào zhě tóng yú dào dé zhě tóng yú dé shī zhě tóng
故从事于道者，同于道①；德者，同于德；失者，同
yú shī tóng yú dào zhě dào yì dé zhī tóng yú dé zhě dé yì dé zhī tóng
于失。同于道者，道亦得之；同于德者，德亦得之；同
yú shī zhě shī yì dé zhī
于失者，失亦得之。②

注释

① 故从事于道者，同于道：通行本作“故从事于道者，道者同于道”，俞樾等认为“同于道”前的“道者”二字是衍文，帛书本亦无此二字，据此予以删除。

② 同于道者，道亦得之；同于德者，德亦得之；同于失者，失亦得之：通行本作“同于道者，道亦乐得之；同于德者，德亦乐得之；同于失者，失亦乐得之”，各句都有“乐”字，疑是诠释性增补，而帛书本、傅奕本等则无“乐”字，据此予以删除。通行本本章末还有“信不足焉，有不信焉”一句，与第十七章重复，疑是错简重出，故予以删除。

今译

少言语合乎自然。所以，狂风刮不了整个早晨，暴雨也不会持续一整天。是谁造成这种现象的？是天地。天地尚且不能持久，何况是人呢？

所以，修道的人，其行为合于道；修德的人，其行为合于德；失去道和德的人，其行为同于失道失德。合于道的人，道与他同在；合于德的人，德与他同在；失道失德的人，失败与他同在。

英译

Speaking little is natural. A violent wind does not last a whole morning, and a torrential rain does not last a whole day. Who causes these? Heaven and Earth. Even Heaven and Earth cannot make their acts last long, let alone human beings.

Therefore, for those who engage in the pursuit of Dao, their actions conform to Dao; for those who engage in the pursuit of De, their actions conform to De; and for those who have lost Dao and De, their actions are in accordance with the state of having lost Dao and De. For those who are embraced by Dao, Dao will be with them; for those who are embraced by De, De will be with them; for those who have lost Dao and De, failure will be with them.

本章主旨

以"希言自然"为核心，借"飘风不终朝，骤雨不终日"的自然现象，强调自然的无为法则及不可抗拒性。倡导人们要与道同行，与德相伴，这样会助力有所成就，而失道失德，则会承受失败的后果。

The gist of the chapter

With "speaking little is natural" as the core, the natural phenomenon of "a violent wind does not last a whole morning, nor does a torrential rain last a whole day" illustrates the principle of natural non-interference, as a fundamental law of the universe that is both inherent and beyond human resistance. Advocating that people should align their lives with Dao and stay accompanied by De will serve as a guiding light on the journey to achieving success, while losing Dao and De will suffer the consequences of failure.

本章启示

顺应自然规律，不过度干预事物发展，无论是教育、管理等都应顺势而为；遵循“道”与“德”行事，坚守道德准则，长远看会获得积极回报；保持诚信，以此增强个人与组织公信力，赢得他人信任；以平和心态面对得失，将其视为事物发展常态，从容应对挫折。

The enlightenment of the chapter

Comply with the laws of nature and refrain from over-interfering with the development of things. Whether in education, management, etc., one should act in accordance with the trend. Act in accordance with the principles of Dao and De, adhere to moral guidelines, and in the long run, positive returns will be obtained. Maintain integrity to enhance the credibility of individuals and organizations and win the trust and cooperation of others. Face gains and losses with a peaceful mindset, regard them as the normal state of the development of things, and calmly cope with setbacks.

第二十四章

qǐ zhě bù lì kuà zhě bù xíng zì xiàn zhě bù míng zì shì zhě bù zhāng
企 者 不 立，跨 者 不 行，自 见 者 不 明，自 是 者 不 彰，
zì fá zhě wú gōng zì jīn zhě bù cháng
自 伐 者 无 功，自 矜 者 不 长。

qí zài dào yě yuē yú shí zhuì xíng wù huò wù zhī gù yǒu dào zhě
其 在 道 也，曰 余 食 赘 行。物 或 恶 之，故 有 道 者
bù chǔ
不 处。

今译

踮起脚后跟的人反而站不稳，大跨步前行的人反而走不远，自我表现（自逞己见）的人反而不得自明，自以为是的人反而不得彰显，自我夸耀的人反而不见功绩，骄傲自大的人反而不能长久。

从道的角度，这种行为是剩饭赘瘤，人们厌恶它，所以有道的人不这样做。

英译

Those who stand on tiptoes are actually unable to stand firm. Those who take big strides forward are actually unable to walk far. Those who show off themselves are actually unable to gain self-understanding. Those who are self-righteous are actually unable to gain prominence. Those who brag about themselves are actually unable to have their achievements recognized. Those who are arrogant and conceited are actually unable to exist for a long time.

From the perspective of Dao, such behaviors are like leftover food and superfluous tumors, which people dislike. Therefore, those who follow Dao do not act in this way.

本章主旨

本章以“企者不立，跨者不行”等现象为喻，告诫人们违背自然规律、急于求成的行为不可持续，强调顺应自然之道的重要性，形成有道与无道的行为对比，引导人们摒弃浮躁自满，以谦逊、踏实的态度行事，遵循道以实现长久发展。

The gist of the chapter

This chapter takes the phenomenon of “Those who stand on tiptoes are actually unable to stand firm. Those who take big strides forward are actually unable to walk far.” as a metaphor, warning people that the behavior that violates the law of nature and is eager to achieve is not sustainable, emphasizing the importance of conforming to the way of nature, forming a contrast between the behavior with Dao and that without Dao, guiding people to abandon impetuous complacency, act with a humble and practical attitude, and follow Dao to achieve long-term development.

本章启示

做事要脚踏实地、循序渐进，不可急于求成；为人应保持谦逊，客观认识自己，避免自我炫耀与自视甚高；要摒弃虚荣，注重实质内容，而非表面风光；时刻遵循正道，以“道”为准则规范言行，坚守正确价值观。

The enlightenment of the chapter

When doing things, one should be down-to-earth and proceed step by step, and not be eager for quick success. As a person, one should remain humble, understand oneself objectively, and avoid self-showing off and being conceited. One should discard vanity and focus on the essence rather than mere appearance. Always follow the right path, take Dao as the criterion to regulate words and deeds, and adhere to the correct values.

第二十五章

yǒu wù hùn chéng xiān tiān dì shēng jì xī liáo xī dú lì ér bù gǎi
有物混成，先天地生。寂兮寥兮，独立而不改，
zhōu xíng ér bù dài kě yǐ wéi tiān dì mǔ wú bù zhī qí míng qiǎng zì zhī yuē
周行而不殆，可以为天地母。吾不知其名，强字之曰
dào qiǎng wéi zhī míng yuē dà dà yuē shì shì yuē yuǎn yuǎn yuē fǎn
道，强为之名曰大。大曰逝，逝曰远，远曰反。

gù dào dà tiān dà dì dà rén yì dà yù zhōng yǒu sì dà ér rén jū
故道大、天大、地大、人亦大①。域中有四大，而人居
qí yī yān rén fǎ dì dì fǎ tiān tiān fǎ dào dào fǎ zì rán
其一焉。人法地，地法天，天法道，道法自然。

注释

① 人亦大：王弼本、河上公本等作“王亦大”，帛书本也作“王亦大”。老子将道、天、地、人作为宇宙间的四大实在，“人亦大”凸显人的主体性，而“王”只是人中的一种。奚桐认为，“古之尊君者妄改之”。故据傅奕本、范应元本等将“王”修正为“人”。

今译

有一个东西浑然一体，在天地出生之前已经存在。它无声无形，独立长存，不可改变，往复运行，永不停止，可以称为天地的母亲。我不知道它的名字，勉强叫它为“道”，勉强取名为“大”。它广大无边而流逝不息，流逝不息而行致遥远，行致遥远而回返本原。

所以说道大、天大、地大、人也大，宇宙中有四大，人是其中之

一。人效法地，地效法天，天效法道，道效法自然（道的运行法则就是自然而然）。

英译

There is something that is an integrated whole, existing before Heaven and Earth. It is soundless and formless, depending on nothing and undergoing no change, moving in a cycle and never ceasing. It can be called the mother of Heaven and Earth. I don't know its name, so I reluctantly call it "Dao", and reluctantly name it "the Great". It is boundless and ceaseless, reaching far away. When it reaches far away, it returns to its origin.

Therefore, Dao is great, Heaven is great, Earth is great, and Man is also great. There are "Four Greats" existences in the universe, and Man is one of them. Man follows the law of Earth, Earth follows the law of Heaven, Heaven follows the law of Dao, and the law of Dao is natural.

本章主旨

本章首先从本体论角度阐述道先于天地的浑然一体、独立、永恒等特性，指出其是宇宙万物根源；接着说明道的广大、循环运行的规律与特征，然后提出宇宙“四大”——道、天、地、人，强调人有重要地位，最后点明人、地、天、道之间的效法关系，核心是“道法自然”，倡导人应顺应自然规律来实现生存与发展。

The gist of the chapter

This chapter first expounds the characteristics of Dao from the perspective of ontology, such as its integrated wholeness, independence, and eternity, which precede the existence of Heaven and Earth, and points out that Dao is the origin of all things in the universe. Then, it explains the laws and characteristics of Dao's boundless, ceaselss and cyclical operation. After that, it puts forward the "Four Greats" in the universe—Dao, Heaven, Earth, and Man, emphasizing the important status of Man. Finally, it clarifies the relationship of emulation among Man, Earth, Heaven, and Dao. The core of it is that "The law of Dao is natural", advocating that Man should conform to Dao to achieve survival and development.

本章启示

要敬畏自然规律，明白"道"为万物根源，依循规律行事以实现人与自然和谐；认识到人类在宇宙中的重要地位与责任，合理利用资源推动发展；顺应自然法则，在生活各领域不过度干预，追求和谐；秉持谦逊态度，承认对"道"认知有限，不断探索、学习。

The enlightenment of the chapter

We should hold nature's laws in awe, understand that Dao is the origin of all things, and act in accordance with these laws to achieve harmony between humanity and nature. Recognize the significant position and responsibilities of humanity in the universe, and make rational use of resources to promote development. Conform to the laws of nature, refrain from excessive intervention in all aspects of life, and pursue harmony. Adopt a humble attitude, acknowledge the limited understanding of Dao, and keep exploring and learning.

第二十六章

zhòng wéi qīng gēn jìng wéi zào jūn shì yǐ shèng rén zhōng rì xíng bù lí
重为轻根，静为躁君。是以圣人[①]终日行不离
zī zhòng suī yǒu róng guān yān chǔ chāo rán nài hé wàn shèng zhī zhǔ ér
辎重，虽有荣观，燕处超然。奈何万乘之主，而
yǐ shēn qīng tiān xià
以身轻天下。

qīng zé shī gēn zào zé shī jūn
轻则失根，躁则失君。

注释

① 圣人：景龙碑本、傅奕本等作“君子”，意指“卿大夫”。《道德经》主要是以“圣人”的品行修为作为效法榜样，故据王弼本、河上公本等校正。

今译

稳重是轻率的根本，笃静是躁动的主宰。所以，圣人整天行动都离不开载重的车辆，虽有华丽的生活，却能安居超然。为何拥有万辆兵车的大国君主还轻率地治理天下？

轻率就会失去根本，躁动就会失去主宰。

英译

The heavy is the root of the light, and the still is the master of restless. Therefore, the sage travels all day without leaving his baggage wagon. Despite a luxurious life, he can live in peace and stay aloof. Why should the ruler of a large state with ten thousand chariots govern the world lightly?

Acting lightly will lead to the loss of the root, and being restless will lead to the loss of the master.

本章主旨

本章老子强调了个人修养中保持稳重和静定的重要性。圣人能够坚守自己的操行和本质，不为物质享受所迷惑，保持一种超然物外的心态。统治者肩负着治理天下的重任，应持守稳重和谨慎的态度对待自己的职责，以修身为治国之本。为人处世和治国理政，应避免轻浮和急躁。

The gist of the chapter

In this chapter, Laozi emphasizes the importance of maintaining stability and stillness in personal cultivation. Sages can stick to their own conduct and essence, not be deceived by material enjoyment, and maintain a detached mentality. Rulers shoulder the heavy responsibility of governing the world, and should treat their duties with a steady and cautious attitude, and take self-cultivation as the foundation of governing the country. In dealing with people and governing the country, one should avoid the light and the restless.

本章启示

行事要注重根基，保持稳重，避免轻率，为长远发展筑牢基础；面对诱惑与繁杂，保持冷静，克制浮躁情绪，以理智分析判断；不被虚荣迷惑，坚守本心，专注内心真实需求与价值；无论处于何位，都要重视责任，谨慎对待事务，不因轻率、浮躁酿恶果。

The enlightenment of the chapter

When taking actions, one should focus on the foundation, remain steady, and avoid restlessness, thus laying a solid groundwork for long-term development. When confronted with temptations and complexities, stay calm, suppress impetuous emotions, and make rational analyses and judgments. Don't be bewitched by vanity; hold fast to your original intention and concentrate on your true inner needs and values. Regardless of your current position, attach importance to your responsibilities, handle matters with caution, and avoid bringing about disastrous consequences due to flippancy and restlessness.

第二十七章

shàn xíng wú zhé jì shàn yán wú xiá zhé shàn shǔ bù yòng chóu cè
善行无辙迹，善言无瑕谪，善数不用筹策，
shàn bì wú guān jiàn ér bù kě kāi shàn jié wú shéng yuē ér bù kě jiě
善闭无关楗而不可开，善结无绳约而不可解。

shì yǐ shèng rén héng shàn jiù rén gù wú qì rén héng shàn jiù wù gù
是以圣人恒善救人，故无弃人；恒善救物，故
wú qì wù shì wèi xí míng
无弃物。是谓袭明。

gù shàn rén zhě bù shàn rén zhī shī bù shàn rén zhě shàn rén zhī zī
故善人者，不善人之师；不善人者，善人之资。
bù guì qí shī bù ài qí zī suī zhì dà mí shì wèi yào miào
不贵其师，不爱其资，虽智大迷，是谓要妙。

今译

善于行走的人，不留下车辙痕迹。善于言谈的人，说话没有瑕疵和过失。擅长计数的人，不需要借助计算筹码。善于关闭门户的人，即使不用栓销，也使人无法打开。善于打结的人，即使不用绳索，也使人无法解开。

圣人总是善于挽救人（人尽其才），所以没有被遗弃的人；总是善于物尽其用，所以没有被废弃的物。这就叫保持道明。

善于行事之人可以作为不善于行事之人的老师，不善于行事之人可以作为善于行事之人的鉴资。不尊重他的老师，不珍惜他的鉴资，虽自以为聪明，其实是大糊涂。这就是精深微妙的道理。

英译

Those who are good at traveling leave no tracks or traces. Those who are good at speaking make no slips or flaws. Those who are good at counting need no counting chips. Those who are good at closing doors can keep them unopenable without bolts. Those who are good at tying knots can make them unbreakable without ropes.

The sages are always good at saving people (making the best use of everyone's talents), so there are no people who are abandoned. The sages are always good at making the best use of things, so there are no things that are discarded. This is called following the wisdom of Dao.

The virtuous can be teachers for the unvirtuous, and the unvirtuous can be a cautionary mirror for the virtuous. Those who don't value their teachers or cherish their mirrors, though seemingly smart, are actually ignorant. This is the profound and subtle truth.

本章主旨

本章是对于自然无为思想的引申。善行、善言、善数、善闭、善结是一种顺应自然、无为而治的智慧。这不仅是一种哲学思想，更是一种生活态度和行为准则。对理解后的行为，有道者能够以顺其自然的智慧，去观照人与物，了解人各有才、物各有用，做到人尽其才、物尽其用。

The gist of the chapter

This chapter is an extension of the thought of being natural and non-interefence. Being good at traveling, speaking, counting, closing doors and tying knots is a kind of wisdom that conforms to nature and governs by non-interference. This is not only a philosophical thought, but also a life attitude and code of conduct. For the behavior after understanding, those who follow Dao can use the wisdom of going with nature to observe people and things, understand that each person has talents and things have their uses, so that people can make the best use of their talents and things.

本章启示

做事追求自然完美境界，让行为、言语等不着痕迹且无瑕疵；秉持包容惜物态度，看到人与物的价值，不抛弃，充分挖掘其潜力并合理利用；辩证看待善恶，以他人为镜，学习长处、反思不足；重视学习来源，尊重教导，珍视经验，汲取智慧，助力成长发展。

The enlightenment of the chapter

When doing things, pursue the realm of natural perfection, making your actions, words, etc. leave no trace and be flawless. Adopt an inclusive and resource-cherishing attitude, recognize the value of people and things, refrain from discarding them, fully tap their potential and make rational use of them. View good and evil dialectically, take others as a mirror, learn from their strengths and reflect on your own shortcomings. Attach importance to the sources of learning, respect teachings, cherish experiences, draw wisdom from them, and facilitate your growth and development.

第二十八章

zhī qí xióng shǒu qí cí wéi tiān xià xī wéi tiān xià xī héng dé bù lí fù guī yú yīng ér
知其雄，守其雌，为天下溪。为天下溪，恒德不离，复归于婴儿。

zhī qí bái shǒu qí hēi wéi tiān xià shì wéi tiān xià shì héng dé bù tè fù guī yú wú jí
知其白，守其黑，为天下式。为天下式，恒德不忒，复归于无极。

zhī qí róng shǒu qí rǔ wéi tiān xià gǔ héng dé nǎi zú fù guī yú pǔ
知其荣，守其辱，为天下谷，恒德乃足，复归于朴。

pǔ sàn zé wéi qì shèng rén yòng zhī zé wéi guān zhǎng gù dà zhì bù gē
朴散则为器，圣人用之，则为官长。故大制不割。

今译

深知雄强，却安守雌柔，这样的人就能成为天下的溪谷（像溪谷一样谦卑低下）。作为天下的溪谷，永恒的德便不会离去，进而回归到婴儿般纯真的状态。

深知明亮，却安守暗昧，这样的人就能成为天下的榜样。成为天下的榜样，永恒的德便不会出现差错，进而回归到无极的境界。

深知荣耀，却安守屈辱，这样的人就能成为天下的川谷。成为天下的川谷，永恒的德便能充足，进而回归到道的真朴状态。

道的真朴状态分散而形成世间万物，圣人善于运用它们从而成为百官之长治理天下。所以，伟大的治理不会去宰割万物。

英译

One who understands the masculinity and strength but keeps to the femininity and gentleness can become the creek of the world (as humble as a creek). Being the creek of the world, the eternal De will never depart, and then one will return to the innocent state of an infant.

One who understands the white but keeps to the black can become a model for the world. Being a model for the world, the eternal De will never go wrong, and then one will return to the state of the infinite.

One who understands the glory but keeps to humiliation can become the valley of the world. Being the valley of the world, the eternal De will be sufficient, and then one will return to the natural simplicity.

When the natural simplicity of Dao disperses and turns into all things in the world, sages make use of it and become the leaders of officials to govern the world. Therefore, great governance will not dissect and manipulate all things.

本章主旨

本章的核心是“复归于朴”，即回归到最原始、最质朴的状态。老子提倡守柔、处下、谦卑的处世哲学，认为这样才能与“道”相合，达到真正的和谐与圆满。圣人治理天下也应顺应自然，保持质朴，不破坏万物的本性。

The gist of the chapter

The core of this chapter is “returning to the natural simplicity”, i. e., returning to the most primitive and simple state. Laozi advocates the philosophy of being soft and humble, believing that this can be in harmony with Dao and achieves the true harmony and perfection. Sages governing the world should also conform to Dao, maintain natural simplicity, and not destroy the natural state of all things.

本章启示

保持谦逊，不恃强，涵养品德，赢得支持合作；以退为进，面对复杂局面冷静观察，把握全局，如商业竞争中兼顾优劣制定策略；淡泊名利，不被虚荣利益左右，回归质朴纯真状态；遵循自然规律，不过度干预，给事物留有发展空间，实现整体和谐，如政府依规律制定政策。

The enlightenment of the chapter

Maintain humility, refrain from relying on strength, cultivate virtue, and thus win support and cooperation. Use the strategy of retreating in order to advance. When facing complex situations, keep to the state of stillness, grasp the overall situation, just like formulating strategies that take into account both advantages and disadvantages in business competition. Be indifferent to fame and fortune, not be swayed by vanity and interests, and return to a simple and innocent state. When governing, follow the law of Dao, avoid over-intervention, give room for the development of things, and achieve overall harmony, just as the government formulates policies in accordance with the law of Dao.

第二十九章

jiāng yù qǔ tiān xià ér wéi zhī　wú jiàn qí bù dé yǐ　tiān xià shén qì　bù
将欲取天下而为之，吾见其不得矣[①]。天下神器，不
kě wéi yě　bù kě zhí yě　wéi zhě bài zhī　zhí zhě shī zhī　shì yǐ shèng rén wú
可为也，不可执也。为者败之，执者失之。是以圣人无
wéi　gù wú bài　wú zhí　gù wú shī
为，故无败；无执，故无失。[②]

fú wù huò xíng huò suí　huò xū huò chuī　huò qiáng huò léi　huò zài huò
夫物或行或随[③]，或歔或吹，或强或羸，或载或
huī　shì yǐ shèng rén qù shèn　qù shē　qù tài
隳。是以圣人去甚、去奢、去泰。

注释

① 古代“已”与“矣”通用，为避免对“不得已”的误读误解，据安伦等校勘，改用“不得矣”。

② 通行本中“是以圣人无为，故无败；无执，故无失”在第六十四章的中间段落，但与该章上下文语义、逻辑毫无关联，疑是错置，而与本章“为者败之，执者失之”文义紧密，逻辑关联，故调整至本章。

③ 夫物或行或随：通行本作“故物或行或随”，此句与上文并无因果关系，按景龙碑本将其修正为“夫”。

今译

如果有人试图通过刻意妄为来掌控天下，我看他是不会成功的。天下是神圣的东西，不可以被掌控，也无法被据为己有。试图掌控它的人必定会失败；试图据有它的人必定会失去它。所以，圣人不做刻意妄为

的事，因此不会遭遇失败；不试图据有什么，所以也不会遭受损失。

（世人性情不一）有的行前，有的随后；有的缓慢，有的急切；有的刚健，有的羸弱；有的自爱，有的堕落。因此，圣人要去除极端、奢侈和过度的行为。

英译

If someone attempts to control the world by forceful means, I don't think he will succeed. The world is a sacred thing that cannot be controlled, nor can it be possessed. Those who try to control it are bound to fail, and those who try to possess it are bound to lose it. Therefore, sages do not engage in forceful means, and thus they will not encounter failure; they do not attempt to possess anything, and thus they will not suffer losses.

(People have different temperaments.) Some walk ahead, while others follow behind; some are laid-back, while others are quick-tempered; some are strong, while others are weak; some cherish themselves, while others degenerate. Therefore, sages should get rid of extreme, extravagant and excessive behaviors.

本章主旨

本章的核心是“无为而治”。老子认为，天下是一个复杂而神圣的整体，不能通过人为的强力或控制来治理。试图强行改变或控制天下，只会导致失败。真正的治理应顺应自然，摒弃极端和过度，保持适度与平衡。

The gist of the chapter

The core of this chapter is "governing by non-interference". Laozi believes that the world is a sacred thing that cannot be governed by forceful means. Attempting to forcibly change or control the world will only lead to failure. True governance should conform to nature, discard extremes and excesses, and maintain harmony and balance.

本章启示

行事须尊重规律，避免强行干预，如保护生态就要顺应自然，不可妄为；要认识并包容事物的多样性，尊重个体差异，如团队合作利用成员不同优势；秉持适度原则，摒弃极端，无论是消费还是处事，都应避免过度与过激。

The enlightenment of the chapter

When taking actions, we should respect the laws and avoid forced intervention. For example, in ecological protection, we should conform to nature and avoid acting recklessly. We need to recognize and embrace the diversity of things, respecting individual differences. Just like in teamwork, we should make use of the talents of team members. Adhere to the principle of harmony and abandon extremes. Whether in consumption or handling affairs, we should avoid excess and over-reaction.

第三十章

yǐ dào zuǒ rén zhǔ zhě bù yǐ bīng qiáng tiān xià qí shì hǎo huán shī zhī
以道佐人主者，不以兵强天下。其事好还。师之

suǒ chǔ jīng jí shēng yān dà jūn zhī hòu bì yǒu xiōng nián
所处，荆棘生焉；大军之后，必有凶年。

shàn zhě guǒ ér yǐ bù yǐ qǔ qiáng guǒ ér wù jīn guǒ ér wù fá
善者果而已，不以取强[①]。果而勿矜，果而勿伐，

guǒ ér wù jiāo guǒ ér bù dé yǐ shì wèi guǒ ér wù qiáng
果而勿骄，果而不得已，是谓果而勿强[②]。

注释

① 不以取强：王弼本作“不敢以取强”。据俞樾等考证，“敢”为衍文，故据景龙碑本、帛书本等校定。

② 是谓果而勿强：通行本等作“果而勿强”。此句是对前面四句的总结，故据景龙碑本、帛书本、竹简本等校定。通行本、帛书本等本章末还有“物壮则老，是谓不道，不道早已”一句，但与其他部分无语义关联，疑是与第五十五章错简重出，据此删除。

今译

用道辅佐君主的人，不靠兵力在天下逞强，因为用兵这件事往往会有报应。军队所到之处，会荆棘丛生。大战之后，必定会出现荒年。

有道之人使用武力，只是为了达到必要的目的，而不是为了逞强。达到目的而不居功自傲，达到目的而不自我夸耀，达到目的而不骄纵轻狂，达到目的只是因为迫不得已。这就叫作达到目的却不逞强。

英译

Those who assist a monarch with Dao do not show off their military force in the world, for using military force often brings about retribution. Wherever the army goes, thorns and brambles will grow abundantly. After a large-scale war, years of famine are bound to follow.

Those who follow Dao use military force only to achieve necessary objectives, rather than to show off their force. They achieve their goals without being self-conceited, without being boastful, and without being arrogant. They resort to military force only when there is no other alternative. This is what is called achieving the goal without showing off their force.

本章主旨

这一章的核心是“反对武力与暴力，顺应‘道’的原则”。老子认为，用“道”的原则辅佐君主，应避免使用武力和战争，因为武力会带来反噬和灾难。真正的智慧是达到目的而不逞强，保持谦逊和节制，避免过度追求强大。

The gist of the chapter

The core of this chapter is "to oppose military force and violence, and to conform to the law of Dao". Laozi believes that following Dao to assist the monarch should avoid the use of force and war, because military force will bring backlash and disaster. True wisdom is to achieve goals without being arrogant, maintain humility and moderation, and avoid excessive pursuit of power.

本章启示

倡导和平理念，无论是国际事务还是日常人际关系交往，都应避免轻易动武，以和平协商解决争端；做事适可而止，取得成果后不骄傲自满、不自我夸耀，保持克制与谦逊，稳步发展。

The enlightenment of the chapter

Advocate the concept of peace. Whether in international affairs or daily interpersonal interactions, one should avoid resorting to force easily and resolve disputes through peaceful negotiations. When doing things, know when to stop. After achieving results, do not be arrogant, complacent, or self-boastful. Maintain restraint and humility, and develop steadily.

第三十一章

fú bīng zhě　bù xiáng zhī qì　wù huò wù zhī　gù yǒu dào zhě bù chǔ
夫兵者①，不祥之器。物或恶之，故有道者不处。
jūn zǐ jū zé guì zuǒ　yòng bīng zé guì yòu　bīng zhě bù xiáng zhī qì　fēi
君子居则贵左，用兵则贵右。兵者不祥之器，非
jūn zǐ zhī qì　bù dé yǐ ér yòng zhī　tián dàn wéi shàng　shèng ér wù měi
君子之器，不得已而用之，恬淡为上。胜而勿美。
ruò měi zhī　shì lè shā rén yě　fú lè shā rén zhě　zé bù kě dé zhì yú tiān xià
若美之②，是乐杀人也。夫乐杀人者，则不可得志于天下
yǐ
矣。

jí shì shàng zuǒ　xiōng shì shàng yòu　piān jiāng jūn jū zuǒ　shàng jiāng jūn
吉事尚左，凶事尚右。偏将军居左，上将军
jū yòu　yán yǐ sàng lǐ chǔ zhī　shā rén zhī zhòng　yǐ āi bēi lì　zhī　zhàn
居右，言以丧礼处之。杀人之众，以哀悲莅③之；战
shèng　yǐ sàng lǐ chǔ zhī
胜，以丧礼处之。

注释

① 夫兵者：通行本作“夫佳兵者”，“佳兵”疑是语义不通，此处按帛书本等予以修正。

② 若美之：王弼本等作“而美之者”，此处按帛书本、景龙碑本校正，更趋简练。

③ 莅：通行本作“泣”。据朱谦之等考证，“泣”是“莅”的误写，此处按帛书本予以修正。

今译

兵器是不祥之物，人们都厌恶它，所以遵循道的人不使用它。在处理日常事务时，君子以左边为尊；但在用兵打仗时，则以右边为尊。兵器不是君子所应使用的器具，只在不得已时而使用，最好也要淡然处之。即使取得胜利，也不应以此为美。如果以胜利为美，那就是以杀人为乐。那些以杀人为乐的人，是不可能在天下取得成功的。

在吉祥的场合，左边是上位；在凶丧的场合，右边是上位。在军中副将站在左边，主将站在右边。这意味着要用丧礼的仪式来对待军事活动。战争中杀人众多，应以悲痛的心情哀悼；打了胜仗，也应该用丧礼的仪式来对待。

英译

Weapons are inauspicious and loathed by all, so those following Dao avoid them. In daily life, gentlemen favor the left; in war, the right.

Weapons aren't for gentlemen, used only when necessary and with indifference. Victory shouldn't be glorified. To delight in it is to delight in killing, and those delight in killing won't succeed in the world.

On auspicious occasions, the left is superior; on mournful ones, the right. In the army, the deputy general is on the left, the chief on the right, meaning war should be treated like a funeral. With many killed in war, mourn with grief. Treat victory as a funeral, too.

本章主旨

这一章的核心是“反对战争，以悲痛的态度对待武力”。老子认为，战争是不祥之事，与“道”的原则相违背。即使不得已而使用武力，也要以淡然、悲痛的态度对待，不能以胜利为美，更不能以杀人为乐。对待战争应以对待丧礼的态度来处理，反思其带来的灾难和痛苦。

The gist of the chapter

The core of this chapter is "oppose war and treat force with grief". Laozi believes that war is ominous and goes against the principle of Dao. Even if force is used as a last resort, it should be treated with indifference and grief, not with victory as beauty, let alone joy in killing. War should be handled with a funeral attitude, reflecting on the disaster and pain it brings.

本章启示

要崇尚和平，深刻认识到战争是不祥之物，尽可能以和平方式解决争端；若不得已动用武力，必须保持克制，遵循必要限度，避免过度暴力；即便取得胜利，也不可宣扬，应尊重生命，反思战争残酷，珍视和平，培养人道主义精神。

The enlightenment of the chapter

We should advocate peace, deeply recognize that war is an inauspicious thing, and resolve disputes through peaceful means whenever possible. If the use of force is inevitable, we must exercise restraint, adhere to the necessary limits, and avoid excessive violence. Even if victory is achieved, it should not be flaunted. Instead, we should respect life, reflect on the brutality of war, cherish peace, and cultivate the spirit of humanism.

第三十二章

dào héng wú míng pǔ　suī xiǎo　tiān xià mò néng chén　hóu wáng ruò
道恒无名朴，虽小①，天下莫能臣。侯王若
néng shǒu zhī　wàn wù jiāng zì bīn
能守之，万物将自宾。

tiān dì xiāng hé　yǐ jiàng gān lù　mín mò zhī lìng ér zì jūn　shǐ zhì yǒu
天地相合，以降甘露，民莫之令而自均。始制有
míng　míng yì jì yǒu　fú yì jiāng zhī zhī　zhī zhī kě yǐ bù dài　pì dào zhī
名，名亦既有，夫亦将知之②，知之可以不殆。譬道之
zài tiān xià　yóu chuān gǔ zhī yú jiāng hǎi
在天下，犹川谷之于江海。

注释

① 道恒无名朴，虽小：通行本作“道恒无名，朴虽小”的断句，“朴虽小”疑是上下文义不通。此处采用高亨等的断句，且与第三十七章“无名之朴”一致。

② 知之：王弼本、帛书乙本等作“知止”，意思是“知道行事的限度，适可而止”。据安伦等校勘，“始制有名”是指“道”开始有名，“知之”是指知晓“道”，且与本章起始句“道恒无名朴”及本章末“譬道之在天下”前后呼应，更符合老子原意，故据此校正。

今译

道永远处于无名而质朴的状态。它虽然幽微不可见，看似渺小，但天下没有谁能使它臣服。如果诸侯、君王能够遵循道（依道来治理天下，不妄为、不扰民，顺应自然规律），那么万物将会自然地归从、宾

服于他。

天地间阴阳之气相互交融，就会降下甘露，人们不需要去指令它，它自然就会均匀地润泽万物。道开始有了名称，既然有了名称，人们就以此知晓道，知晓道就可以避免危险。道存在于天下万物，就如同百川之水汇聚于江海一样（天下万物都会自然而然地归向于道）。

英译

Dao is ever nameless. Despite its seeming plainness and triviality, nothing under Heaven can subdue it. If rulers abide by it, all things will spontaneously submit.

When Heaven and Earth interact, sweet dew descends, naturally nourishing all things evenly without need for instruction. Once Dao has a name, people can understand it thereby. Once understanding it, they can avoid danger. Dao pervades all under Heaven, much like rivers flowing into the sea (all under Heaven will naturally return to Dao).

本章主旨

这一章主要阐述了“道”的无名、质朴、渺小却又无比强大的特性，强调了侯王应守道以治天下，同时通过自然现象和比喻，说明了道在宇宙万物中的重要地位和作用，体现了老子对自然、社会和人生的深刻思考。

The gist of the chapter

This chapter mainly expounds the nameless, simple, trivial but incomparably powerful characteristics of Dao, emphasizing that lords and kings should keep Dao to rule the world. At the same time, through natural phenomena and metaphors, it explains the important position and role of Dao in all things in the universe, reflecting Laozi's profound thinking about nature, society and people's life.

本章启示

要敬畏并遵循自然规律，认识其不可抗拒性；管理上倡导无为而治，减少干预，让事物自然发展，激发活力；在追求各类目标时懂得知止，把握分寸，避免因过度而陷入困境；认识到道统领万物，追求人与人、人与社会、人与自然的和谐统一。

The enlightenment of the chapter

We should hold the laws of nature in awe and abide by them, recognizing their irresistibility. In management, we advocate governing by non-interference, reducing intervention, allowing things to develop naturally, and stimulating vitality. When pursuing various goals, we should know when to stop, maintain proper moderation, and avoid being overly trapped in difficulties. We should realize that Dao governs all things and strive for the harmonious unity among people, between people and society, and between people and nature.

第三十三章

zhī rén zhě zhì zì zhī zhě míng shèng rén zhě yǒu lì zì shèng zhě qiáng zhī zú zhě fù qiáng xíng zhě yǒu zhì bù shī qí suǒ zhě jiǔ sǐ ér bù wáng zhě shòu

知人者智，自知者明。胜人者有力，自胜者强。知足者富。强行者有志。不失其所者久。死而不亡者寿。

今译

了解别人的人是聪慧的，而了解自己的人才是明智的。战胜别人的人有力量，战胜自己的人才是真正强大的。知道满足的人是富有的。做事坚持不懈的人有意志力。不丧失根基的人能够长久。身死而精神不亡的人才算得上长寿。

英译

Those who understand others are smart, but those who understand themselves are enlightened. Those who defeat others are strong, yet those who overcome themselves are powerful. Those content with what they have are rich. Those who persevere have willpower. Those who stay true to their roots endure. Those whose spirit lives on after death achieve true longevity.

本章主旨

这一章主要从个人修养的角度阐述了老子对于智慧、力量、富有、志向、长久和长寿的独特理解，强调了自知、自胜、知足等内在品质的重要性，为人们提供了一种独特的人生哲学和价值取向。

The gist of the chapter

This chapter mainly expounds Laozi's unique understanding of wisdom, strength, wealth, ambition, endurance, and longevity from the perspective of personal cultivation, emphasizing the importance of inner qualities such as knowing himself, self-control, and self-contentment, and providing people with a unique philosophy of life and value orientation.

本章启示

注重自我认知，了解自己比了解他人更重要，有助于找准人生方向；强调战胜自我，克服自身弱点实现成长，成为真正强者；倡导知足常乐，珍惜拥有，同时坚持力行以实现志向；鼓励坚守原则信念，追求精神价值，实现超越生命的永恒。

The enlightenment of the chapter

Emphasize self-awareness. Understanding oneself is more important than understanding others, which can help identify the right direction in life. Stress the importance of overcoming oneself. Overcoming one's own weaknesses to achieve growth makes one a true powerful person. Advocate being content with what one has and finding joy in it. Cherish what one has while persevering in taking action to fulfill one's aspirations. Adhere to the principles and beliefs, pursuing spiritual values, and achieving an eternity that transcends life.

第三十四章

dà dào fàn xī qí kě zuǒ yòu wàn wù shì zhī yǐ shēng ér bù cí gōng
大道泛兮，其可左右。万物恃之以生而不辞①，功
chéng ér bù yǒu yī yǎng wàn wù ér bù wéi zhǔ kě míng yú xiǎo wàn wù
成而不有。衣养万物而不为主，可名于小②。万物
guī yān ér bù wéi zhǔ kě míng wéi dà yǐ qí zhōng bù zì wéi dà gù néng
归焉而不为主，可名为大。以其终不自为大，故能
chéng qí dà
成其大。

tiān xià jiē wèi wǒ dào dà sì bù xiào fú wéi dà gù sì bù xiào ruò
天下皆谓我：道大，似不肖。夫唯大，故似不肖。若
xiào jiǔ yǐ qí xì yě fú
肖，久矣其细也夫。③

注释

① 辞：此处解释为"推辞"，也有注本解释为"言辞"或"止息"。

② 通行本在"可名于小"前还有"常无欲"一句，奚桐、蒋锡昌、严灵峰等认为此句是衍文，不符合"衣养万物而不为主，可名于小。万物归焉而不为主，可名为大"的对文，故删除"常无欲"一句。

③ 通行本"天下皆谓我：道大，似不肖。夫唯大，故似不肖。若肖，久矣其细也夫。"原在第六十七章开头位置，但与该章其他部分无语义和逻辑关联，疑是错简误置。但与本章有语义和逻辑关联，此处按安伦的校勘，将其调整至本章。

今译

大道泛漫于天下，左右无所不在。万物依赖它生长而不推辞，有了功绩也不居功和占有。它养育万物而不自以为主宰，因此可以称它为“小”。万物归附于它也不自以为主宰，所以又可以称它为“大”。正因为它从不自以为大，所以才能成就它的“大”。

天下人都对我说：道宏大，似乎没有什么具体的东西可以与之相似。正因为它宏大，所以才似乎不像任何具体的事物。如果它像某个具体的东西，那它早就变得渺小了。

英译

The Great Dao pervades all, left and right. All things live by it, yet it never shirks. It accomplishes all things without claiming the credits. It nurtures all things without being their master, hence it can be called “Small”. All things submit to it, yet it still doesn’t claim mastery, thus it can be called “Great”. Because it never asserts itself as great, its greatness is truly achieved.

All under Heaven tell me: Dao is great, but it does not look like anything. It is just because it is so great that it does not look like anything. If it had looked like anything, it would have been trivial long ago.

本章主旨

本章通过对大道的描述，进一步阐述了道的特性和作用，强调了道的无私、无欲、无为及不居功自傲的品质，揭示了道之所以伟大的根本原因在于其谦逊和不自以为是的本质。正因为道的宏大和无所不包，所以无法用任何具体的事物来比拟和形容它。如果它能够被具体地描述或等同于某个具体的东西，那么它就失去了其作为道的宏大和普遍性，而变得狭隘和渺小了。

The gist of the chapter

This chapter further expounds Dao's characteristics and functions by depicting it, highlighting Dao's selflessness, lack of desire, non-interference, and modesty. It reveals that Dao's greatness stems from its humble and selfless nature. Precisely due to its vastness and all-inclusiveness, Dao cannot be compared to or described by any specific thing. If it could be specifically defined or equated with something, it would lose its grand and universal essence as Dao and become trivial.

本章启示

倡导无私奉献，如道滋养万物般助人且不图回报；强调低调谦逊，即便成就非凡也不居功自傲，以赢得尊重并持续进步；提倡胸怀宽广，像道包容万物一样，接纳不同的人和观念，促进合作与社会和谐；鼓励坚守初心，淡泊名利，不为功名利禄所扰，专注自身成长与贡献。

The enlightenment of the chapter

Advocate selfless dedication, helping others like Dao nourishes all without seeking return. Stress being low-key and modest, claiming no credit even after great achievements, to earn respect and keep advancing. Advocate an open mind, accepting diverse people and ideas as Dao embraces all, for better cooperation and social harmony. Encourage staying true to one's original aspiration, being indifferent to fame and wealth, undistracted by material gains and honors, and focusing on personal growth and contributions.

第三十五章

zhí dà xiàng tiān xià wǎng wǎng ér bù hài ān píng tài
执大象，天下往。往而不害，安平太。

lè yǔ ěr guò kè zhǐ dào zhī chū kǒu dàn hū qí wú wèi shì zhī bù zú
乐与饵，过客止。道之出口，淡乎其无味。视之不足

jiàn tīng zhī bù zú wén yòng zhī bù kě jì
见，听之不足闻，用之不可既①。

注释

① 用之不可既：王弼本等作“用之不足既”。“不可既”指道的作用不可穷尽，此处按帛书本、竹简本等予以校正。

今译

执守大道，天下人都来归附投靠。归附投靠而互不伤害，天下就能和平、安宁。

音乐和美食，能使过路的人都为之停步。用言语来表述大道，是淡然无味的，看它看不见，听它也听不见，而它的作用却无穷无尽。

英译

Hold fast to the Great Dao, all under Heaven will come to you. When people come together in this way, ceasing to harm one another, people can enjoy safety and peace.

Music and delicious food can entice passers-by to stop. When spoken of, Dao seems insipid and tasteless. Look at it, and it cannot be seen. Listen to it, and it cannot be heard. Use it, and it is inexhaustible.

本章主旨

这一章主要是通过对比“乐与饵”的短暂诱惑和“道”的平淡却无穷的特质，强调了“道”的重要性和价值，提醒人们不要被外在的声色犬马等表面的东西迷惑，而要追求和遵循“道”，以达到社会的和谐与个人的长久发展。

The gist of the chapter

This chapter mainly emphasizes the importance and value of Dao by contrasting the short-lived temptation of “music and delicacies” with the dull but endless characteristics of Dao, reminding people not to be fooled by external superficial things such as sensual pleasures and temptations, but to pursue and follow Dao in order to achieve social harmony and long-term personal development.

本章启示

个人与领导者应坚守道的原则，以正确理念引领行为，实现个人发展与社会和谐；保持清醒，不被如音乐、美食般的世俗短暂引诱迷惑，着眼长远，追求真正价值；不以貌取“道”，学会透过表象挖掘如“道”般的事物的内在价值，不轻视平凡事物与低调之人。

The enlightenment of the chapter

Individuals and leaders should abide by the principles of Dao, steer their actions with proper concepts, and foster personal growth and social harmony. Remain clear-headed, resisting the allure of short-term worldly temptations such as music and delicacies, and concentrate on the long-term quest for true value. Don't assess Dao by its outward appearance. Learn to discern the profound inner worth of things, akin to that of Dao, beneath their surface. Never despise ordinary things or mundane people.

第三十六章

jiāng yù xī zhī bì gù zhāng zhī jiāng yù ruò zhī bì gù qiáng zhī jiāng
将欲歙之，必固张之。将欲弱之，必固强之。将
yù fèi zhī bì gù xīng zhī jiāng yù qǔ zhī bì gù yǔ zhī shì wèi wēi míng
欲废之，必固兴之。将欲取之，必固与之。是谓微明。

róu ruò shèng gāng qiáng yú bù kě tuō yú yuān guó zhī lì qì bù kě yǐ
柔弱胜刚强。鱼不可脱于渊，国之利器不可以
shì rén
示人。

今译

要收缩它，必先让它扩张。要削弱它，必先让它强大。要废除它，必先让它兴盛。要夺取它，必先给予。这就叫作洞察微妙。

柔弱能够战胜刚强。鱼不能离开深渊；国家的利器不可以向人展示。

英译

To contract, first expand; to weaken, first strengthen; to abolish, first promote; to take, first give. This is subtle insight.

The soft prevails over the hard. Fish should stay in deep water, and a state's powerful weapons should remain hidden.

本章主旨

本章体现了老子的辩证法思想，揭示了事物矛盾双方相互依存、相互转化的关系，强调了要以柔克刚、不轻易彰显实力的道理。

The gist of the chapter

This chapter epitomizes Laozi's dialectical thought, reveals the relationship between the interdependence and mutual transformation of the contradictions between things, and emphasizes the principle of overcoming the hard with the soft and without flaunting one's strength readily.

本章启示

洞察事物转化规律，懂得以退为进，如商业谈判时先予后取，为长远成功铺垫；重视柔弱力量，明白以柔克刚道理，如教育孩子用温和方式更有效；学会内敛，个人保守隐私，组织保护机密，如企业严防商业机密泄露，维持自身优势。

The enlightenment of the chapter

Gain an insight into the laws of transformation of things and understand the strategy of retreating in order to advance. For example, in business negotiations, give first and then take, paving the way for long-term success. Attach importance to the power of softness and understand the principle that softness can overcome hardness. For instance, a gentle approach is more effective when educating children. Learn to be reserved. Individuals should keep their privacy confidential, and organizations should safeguard their confidential information. For example, enterprises should take strict precautions against the leakage of business secrets to maintain their competitive advantages.

第三十七章

dào héng wú wéi ér wú bù wéi hóu wáng ruò néng shǒu zhī wàn wù jiāng
道恒无为而无不为，侯王若能守之，万物将
zì huà
自化。

huà ér yù zuò wú jiāng zhèn zhī yǐ wú míng zhī pǔ fú yì jiāng wú yù
化而欲作，吾将镇之以无名之朴[①]，夫亦将无欲。
wú yù yǐ jìng tiān xià jiāng zì dìng
无欲以静，天下将自定。

注释

① 通行本在“吾将镇之以无名之朴”后又另起“无名之朴”一句，疑是重复，此处采用竹简本的表述，不叠此句。

今译

道总是不刻意妄为，却又无所不为。如果诸侯和君王能够遵循道，万物就会自然地归化。

在万物归化的过程中如果产生了贪欲，我就会用道的无名质朴来镇住它，这样就不起贪欲了。不起贪欲而趋于宁静，天下就自然安定了。

英译

Dao never acts with interference, yet there is nothing it cannot do. If rulers abide by it, all things will transform spontaneously.

When desires emerge during this transformation, I will quell them with the Dao's nameless natural simplicity. Then desires vanish. With no desires comes tranquility, and the world will naturally achieve stability.

本章主旨

本章核心是阐述“道”的“无为而无不为”的特性。由“道”的特性延伸到治国理政方面，老子主张侯王要守道，即遵循“无为”的原则来治理国家，这是老子“无为而治”政治思想的重要体现。在万物自然发展过程中可能会出现“欲作”的情况，即人们会产生贪欲等不良欲望，老子认为要用“无名之朴”，也就是“道”的质朴纯真来镇服万物自然发展过程中可能会出现的欲望，通过统治者的“无为而治”和对百姓欲望的合理引导，使社会达到一种自然、和谐、稳定的状态。

The gist of the chapter

This chapter expounds Dao's characteristic of “doing nothing contrived yet achieving everything”. Laozi extended this to state governance, advocating that rulers should follow Dao, governing with non-interference, a key aspect of his political ideology. He noted that during the natural development of all things, desires may arise. Laozi held that the natural simplicity of Dao should be used to regulate this development. When desires emerge, through the ruler's non-contrived governance and properly refraining from people's desires, society will attain a natural, harmonious and stable state.

本章启示

秉持无为理念，在教育、管理等方面不过度干预，给予发展空间；遵循自然规律，如生态保护与市场经济，让事物自行发展；克制欲望，以道的质朴抑制欲念，保持内心平静，构建和谐社会；以道为指引，个人与领导者依道而行，追求和谐有序，实现共同进步。

The enlightenment of the chapter

Uphold the concept of "non-interference". In aspects such as education and management, refrain from excessive interference and provide room for development. Abide by the laws of nature. For example, in ecological protection and the market economy, let things develop on their own. Restrain desires, suppress cravings with the natural simplicity of Dao, maintain inner peace, and build a harmonious society. Guided by Dao, both individuals and leaders should act in accordance with it, pursue harmony and order, and achieve common progress.

第三十八章

shàng dé bù dé shì yǐ yǒu dé xià dé bù shī dé shì yǐ wú dé shàng
上德不德，是以有德；下德不失德，是以无德。上
dé wú wéi ér wú yǐ wéi shàng rén wéi zhī ér wú yǐ wéi shàng yì wéi zhī ér
德无为而无以为①，上仁为之而无以为，上义为之而
yǒu yǐ wéi shàng lǐ wéi zhī ér mò zhī yìng zé rǎng bì ér rēng zhī
有以为，上礼为之而莫之应，则攘臂而扔之。

gù shī dào ér hòu dé shī dé ér hòu rén shī rén ér hòu yì shī yì ér hòu
故失道而后德，失德而后仁，失仁而后义，失义而后
lǐ fú lǐ zhě zhōng xìn zhī bó ér luàn zhī shǒu qián shí zhě dào zhī huá ér
礼。②夫礼者，忠信之薄而乱之首。前识者，道之华而
yú zhī shǐ
愚之始。

shì yǐ dà zhàng fū chǔ qí hòu bù jū qí bó chǔ qí shí bù jū
是以大丈夫处其后，不居其薄；处其实，不居
qí huá
其华。③

注释

① 通行本在“上德无为而无以为”后还有“下德无为而有以为”一句，帛书本则无此句。据安伦等校勘，疑是后人的衍文。

② 故失道而后德，失德而后仁，失仁而后义，失义而后礼：此处解释为“失去了道就会失去德，失去了德就会失去仁，失去了仁就会失去义，失去了义就会失去礼”，也有注本将其解释为“失去道后才有德，失去德后才有仁，失去仁后才有义，失去义后才有礼”。

③ 通行本本章末还有“故去彼取此”一句，同第十二章注解，予以删除。

今译

上德之人不刻意追求德的形式，所以才有德。下德之人刻意不失去德的形式，反而没有德。上德之人不妄为且无意为之，上仁之人有所作为但无意作为，上义之人有所作为且有意为之，上礼之人有所作为但无人回应，于是就伸出手臂强迫别人依从。

因此，失去了道就会失去德，失去了德就会失去仁，失去了仁就会失去义，失去了义就会失去礼。当只剩下礼的时候，忠诚和诚信就变得淡薄了，混乱也就开始了。只知道崇尚礼的人，不过是抓住了道的虚华外表，这是愚昧的开端。

所以，大丈夫立身敦厚而不居于浅薄，立身笃实而不居于浮华。

英译

A man of high De doesn't seek the form of De, yet possesses it. A man of low De tries to maintain the form of De but actually lacks it.

A man of high De takes no artificial actions, for he has no such intent. A man of great benevolence takes actions but without such intent. A man of high righteousness takes actions with intent. A man of high propriety takes actions, yet receives no response, thus he rolls up his sleeves and forcibly drags others to comply.

Therefore, without Dao, one will lose De; without De, one will lose benevolence; without benevolence, one will lose righteousness; and without righteousness, one will lose propriety. When only propriety exists, loyalty and honesty wane and chaos ensues. Focusing on propriety alone is but the veneer of Dao and the onset of ignorance.

Therefore, a great man adheres to the substantial and shuns the superficial, stays with the genuine and avoids the showy.

本章主旨

辨析“上德”“下德”以明“德”之真义，阐述“道”“德”“仁”

“义”“礼”的递失关系以揭示道德衰退，批判当时社会重虚华、缺忠信的现象，倡导人们摒弃浇薄虚华，回归质朴，以达与“道”合一之境。

The gist of the chapter

Distinguish and analyze the true meaning of high De and low De to clarify the true meaning of De, elaborate on the successive loss relationship among Dao, De, benevolence, righteousness and propriety to reveal the moral decline, criticize the then-prevalent social phenomenon of valuing vanity and lacking loyalty and trustworthiness, and advocate that people abandon superficiality and vanity and return to natural simplicity, so as to achieve the state of unity with Dao.

本章启示

追求道德应重本质，回归质朴，真心助人而非图赞誉；警惕道德流于形式，勿仅依赖礼仪，要注重真诚忠信；坚守根本，不被虚华迷惑，如追求成功注重能力与成果；以“道”为核心塑造价值观，个人内化道德，社会倡导“道”的理念，促进和谐进步。

The enlightenment of the chapter

When pursuing high De, one should focus on its essence, return to simplicity, and help others sincerely rather than seeking praise. Be vigilant against De becoming a mere formality. Don’t rely solely on etiquette; instead, emphasize sincerity and faithfulness. Stick to the fundamentals and do not be misled by vanity. For example, when pursuing success, focus on capabilities and achievements. Shape values with Dao at the core. Individuals should internalize De, and society should advocate the concept of Dao to promote harmonious progress.

第三十九章

xī zhī dé yī zhě tiān dé yī yǐ qīng dì dé yī yǐ níng shén dé yī yǐ
昔之得一者：天得一以清，地得一以宁，神得一以
líng gǔ dé yī yǐ yíng wàn wù dé yī yǐ shēng hóu wáng dé yī yǐ wéi tiān
灵，谷得一以盈，万物得一以生，侯王得一以为天
xià zhèng
下正①。

qí zhì zhī yě tiān wú yǐ qīng jiāng kǒng liè dì wú yǐ níng jiāng kǒng fèi
其致之也：天无以清将恐裂，地无以宁将恐废，
shén wú yǐ líng jiāng kǒng xiē gǔ wú yǐ yíng jiāng kǒng jié wàn wù wú yǐ
神无以灵将恐歇，谷无以盈将恐竭，万物无以
shēng jiāng kǒng miè hóu wáng wú yǐ wéi zhèng jiāng kǒng jué
生将恐灭，侯王无以为正②将恐蹶。③

注释

① 以为天下正：王弼本作“以为天下贞”，古代“正”“贞”为通假，此处按河上公本、帛书本等予以校正。

② 侯王无以为正：王弼本作“侯王无以为贵高”，据陈鼓应、安伦等校勘，此处对“贵高”予以修正，且与“侯王得一以为天下正”上下文对应。

③ 通行本本章末还有“故贵以贱为本，高以下为基。是以侯王自称孤、寡、不毂。此非以贱为本邪？非乎？故致誉无誉，不欲碌碌如玉，珞珞如石”一段，但本章阐述的是道与天地万物的关系，而该段所谈及的贵贱高下与本章的文意、逻辑不相关联，疑是与第二章错置。通行本第四十二章原有“人之所恶，唯孤、寡、不毂，而王公以为称。故物或损之而益，或益之而损。人之所教，吾亦教之：‘强梁者不得其

死'。吾将以为教父。"一段，也疑是错置。据安伦等校勘，将其合并调整至第二章的中间段落。

今译

古来得道者：天得道而清明；地得道而宁静；神得道而灵验；河谷得道而充盈；万物得道而生长；侯王得道而使天下安定。

推而言之，天不能保持清明，恐怕要崩裂；地不能保持安宁，恐怕要震溃；神不能保持灵验，恐怕要消失；河谷不能保持充盈，恐怕要干涸；万物不能保持生长，恐怕要灭绝；侯王不能守正，恐怕要倾覆。

英译

Those who attained the One (Dao) in ancient times:
Heaven, with the One, was clear;
Earth, with the One, was tranquil;
Deities, with the One, were efficacious;
Valleys, with the One, were full;
All things, with the One, thrived;
Lords and kings, with the One, stabilized the world.
The reasons are:
Without clarity, Heaven might crack;
Without tranquility, Earth might turn desolate;
Without efficacy, deities might cease;
Without fullness, valleys might dry up;
Without sustenance, all things might perish;
Without justice, lords and kings might fall.

本章主旨

本章指出天、地、神、谷、万物、侯王等世间万类的良好状态与正常运行都得益于道。如天因道而清明，地因道而宁静等，表明"道"是宇宙万物存在和发展的根本依据与内在法则，是维持宇宙秩序与万物和谐的关键力量，凸显了道在老子哲学体系中的核心地位和决定性作用。

The gist of the chapter

It is pointed out in this chapter that the good state and normal operation of all things in the world, such as Heaven, Earth, gods, valleys, all things, and kings, all benefit from Dao. For example, the sky is clear because of Dao, and the earth is tranquil because of Dao, etc., indicating that Dao is the fundamental basis and inner law for the existence and development of all things in the universe, and is the key force for maintaining the order of the universe and the harmony of all things. It highlights the core position and decisive role of Dao in Laozi's philosophical system.

本章启示

无论是个人还是组织，都要坚守“道”这一根本，遵循自然规律和社会法则。比如，个人在成长过程中要坚守道德底线和人生原则，企业发展要遵循市场规律和商业道德，如此才能实现稳定和长久发展。

The enlightenment of the chapter

Whether for individuals or organizations, it is essential to adhere to the fundamental Dao and follow the laws of nature and social rules. For instance, during the growth process, individuals should uphold moral bottom lines and life principles. When it comes to enterprise development, it should abide by market laws and business ethics. Only in this way can stable and long-term development be achieved.

第四十章

fǎn zhě dào zhī dòng ruò zhě dào zhī yòng tiān xià wàn wù shēng yú yǒu
反[1] 者 道 之 动，弱 者 道 之 用。天 下 万 物 生 于有，
yǒu shēng yú wú
有 生 于无。

注释

① 反：在老子哲学中，“反”通常蕴含“相反对立”与“循环往复”这两层意思。

今译

相反和往复是道的运动规律，柔弱是道的作用方式。天下万物都生于有，而有则生于无。

英译

Reversal and cyclical recurrence are the movement of Dao, while softness and weakness are the functions of Dao. All things under Heaven are born from being, and being is born from non-being.

本章主旨

本章阐述了道的运动规律和作用方式，指出其运动规律是循环往复、对立转化，其作用方式是柔弱的，接着阐述了万物由“有”而生，“有”又源于“无”的生成根源。

The gist of the chapter

It expounds the movement law and mode of action of Dao. It points out that Dao's movement law is cyclical reciprocation and opposition-based transformation, and its mode of action is characterized by softness and weakness. It further expounds that all things are born from being, and being itself originates from non-being.

本章启示

用辩证思维看待事物变化，明白逆境藏转机、顺境含危机，居安思危；重视柔弱力量，以温和、柔韧方式解决问题，懂得以柔克刚；理解有无相生，善于从“无”中发现机会创造“有”，在有成果时适时归零，重新出发。

The enlightenment of the chapter

Adopt dialectical thinking to observe the changes of things. Recognize that adversity holds the chance of a turnaround and prosperity hides potential crises. Stay vigilant in times of peace. Value the power of softness, solve problems gently and flexibly, and know that softness prevails over hardness. Grasp that being and non-being are mutually generative. Be adept at seizing opportunities in non-being to create being, and upon achieving success, reset promptly and start afresh.

第四十一章

shàng shì wén dào　qín ér xíng zhī　zhōng shì wén dào　ruò cún ruò wáng
上士闻道，勤而行之；中士闻道，若存若亡；
xià shì wén dào　dà xiào zhī　bù xiào bù zú　yǐ wéi dào
下士闻道，大笑之。不笑不足以为道。

gù jiàn yán yǒu zhī　míng dào ruò mèi　jìn dào ruò tuì　yí dào ruò lèi
故建言有之：明道若昧，进道若退，夷道若颣。
shàng dé ruò gǔ　guǎng dé ruò bù zú　jiàn dé ruò tōu　zhì dé ruò yú　dà bái
上德若谷，广德若不足，建德若偷，质德若渝。大白
ruò rǔ　dà fāng wú yú　dà qì miǎn chéng　dà yīn xī shēng　dà xiàng wú
若辱[1]，大方无隅，大器免成[2]，大音希声，大象无
xíng　dào yǐn wú míng　fú wéi dào　shàn dài qiě chéng
形，道隐无名。夫唯道，善贷且成。

注释

① 大白若辱：本章依次论述“道”、“德”（道的体现和作用）、“大”（道的显现），通行本“大白若辱”原在“上德若谷”与“广德若不足”之间，显得语义、逻辑混乱。据安伦等校勘，调整至“大方无隅”之前，则语序顺畅、体例完整、逻辑严密。

② 大器免成：通行本作“大器晚成”，此处采用帛书本作“大器免成”，更符合“大白若辱，大方无隅，大音希声，大象无形”等排比句中的“大”与“无”的语义对比。

今译

上等士人听闻道，努力践行。中等士人听闻道，半信半疑。下等士

人听闻道，大声嘲笑。如果道不被嘲笑，也就不足以成为道了。

所以古时有这样的说法：光明的道像是暗昧，前进的道像是后退，平坦的道像是崎岖，崇高的德像是低谷，丰沛的德像是不足，刚健的德像是懈怠，纯净的德像是混浊。最大的白好像有黑垢，最大的方没有棱角，最大的器物无须成形，最大的声响听来无声，最大的形象没有形迹。道幽隐而没有名称。然而，只有道善于施与并成就万物。

英译

People of high virtue, upon hearing of Dao, practice it assiduously. Those of moderate virtue, upon hearing of Dao, are half believing and half doubting, while those of inferior virtue laugh at it. If it weren't laughed at, it wouldn't be worthy of being Dao.

Thus, there are old sayings: the bright Dao seems dim; the advancing Dao feels like a retreat; the smooth Dao appears rough. The high De resembles a valley; the abundant De seems lacking; the robust De seems inert; the pure De looks sullied. The sheer white seems black; the greatest square has no corners; the grandest vessel takes no definite form; the great music is faintly heard; the greatest image is formless. Dao is hidden and nameless, yet only Dao is good at bestowing and accomplishing all things.

本章主旨

本章阐述了“道”幽隐无形、与世俗认知相悖的特性，指出不同人对“道”的不同态度，以辩证的视角说明“道”貌似虚无却作用无穷，借此启发人们超越世俗浅见，遵循“道”的规律。

The gist of the chapter

It elaborates on the intangible nature of Dao and its divergence from worldly understanding. It also highlights how people of varying mindsets react to Dao. From a dialectical standpoint, it reveals that though Dao appears void, it possesses boundless power. This aims to encourage people to rise above mundane perspectives and abide by the laws of Dao.

本章启示

认知正确理念后要积极践行，坚定信念付诸行动；不被表象迷惑，洞察事物本质，清醒面对复杂现象；追求成功要不急不躁、厚积薄发，重视长期积累；为人处世应内敛含蓄、低调务实，不炫耀张扬；相信并顺应道的力量，依循规律实现目标。

The enlightenment of the chapter

Once you've grasped the right concepts and vision, act on them actively and with conviction. Don't be deceived by appearances; instead, discern the essence of things and approach complex situations with clarity. When striving for success, remain composed and patient, leveraging your accumulated strength and valuing long-term growth. In interpersonal and practical matters, be modest, understated and down-to-earth, and refrain from ostentation. Have faith in and align with the power of Dao, achieving your goals by adhering to its principles.

第四十二章

dào shēng yī　yī shēng èr　èr shēng sān　sān shēng wàn wù　wàn wù
道生一，一生二，二生三，三生万物。万物
fù yīn ér bào yáng　chōng qì yǐ wéi hé
负阴而抱阳，冲气以为和。①

注释

① 通行本原有“人之所恶，唯孤、寡、不毂，而王公以为称。故物或损之而益，或益之而损。人之所教，吾亦教之：强梁者不得其死。吾将以为教父。”一段，但与上一段语义、逻辑不相关联，疑是错简，故予以删除。

今译

道生成了初始的混沌统一体，这统一体产生出阴阳二气，阴阳二气交合又产生了世间万物。万物都蕴含着阴的一面，又怀抱着阳的一面，阴阳两种力量相互激荡交融，从而达到和谐的状态。

英译

Dao gives birth to One (the initial chaotic unity). The One gives birth to Two (the two vital forces of Yin and Yang). The Two gives birth to Three (the third state generated by the mutual combination of the two vital forces of Yin and Yang). The Three gives birth to all things. All things carry Yin and embrace Yang, and the two forces of Yin and Yang interact and blend, thus attaining a state of harmony.

本章主旨

本章老子阐释了宇宙生成论。道为万物根源，由道生一，一生二，二生三，三生万物，说明道创生万物时的活动历程。

The gist of the chapter

In this chapter, Laozi expounds on the theory of cosmic genesis. Dao, as the root of all things, generates the One, which begets the Two, then the Three, and finally all things, depicting the process of the Dao's creation of all things.

本章启示

认识事物依循道衍生的发展规律，从宏观把握整体趋势；秉持阴阳平衡观念，在工作生活、人际关系等方面追求和谐发展。

The enlightenment of the chapter

When perceiving things, comprehend the developmental laws from Dao and grasp the overall trend macroscopically. Adhere to the concept of Yin-Yang balance and pursue harmonious development in work, life, and interpersonal relations.

第四十三章

tiān xià zhī zhì róu chí chěng tiān xià zhī zhì jiān wú yǒu rù wú jiàn wú shì
天下之至柔，驰骋天下之至坚，无有入无间。吾是
yǐ zhī wú wéi zhī yǒu yì bù yán zhī jiào wú wéi zhī yì tiān xià xī jí zhī
以知无为之有益。不言之教，无为之益，天下希及之。

今译

天下至柔之物可以驾驭天下至坚之物，无形的东西可以穿透没有间隙的东西。由此我领悟到无为的益处。无言的教化、无为的益处，世上鲜有人能理解并践行。

英译

The softest under Heaven masters the hardest; the formless penetrates the seamless. Thus I know the benefits of "wu-wei" (non-action). Wordless teaching and the merits of "wu-wei" (non-action) are rarely grasped and practiced in the world.

本章主旨

老子以“天下之至柔，驰骋天下之至坚”“无有入无间”等对自然现象的观察和思考，阐述了最柔弱的东西能穿透最坚硬之物，无形力量可穿透无间隙之物的道理，深入阐述了“柔”“无为”“不言之教”等思想观念。这些思想相互关联，共同构成了老子哲学中独特的价值观和方法论。

The gist of the chapter

Through observing and reflecting on natural phenomena like "The softest under Heaven masters the hardest, and the formless penetrates the seamless", Laozi expounded the principle that the weakest can pierce the strongest and the invisible force can permeate the gapless. He delved into concepts such as "softness", "wu-wei" (non-action) and "wordless teaching". These ideas are interconnected, forming the unique values and methodology within Laozi's philosophy.

本章启示

面对困难强敌，善于以柔克刚，发挥柔性力量，如温和沟通促谈判成功；洞察无形力量，重视无为作用，顺应规律，如教育孩子时给予其自由，促进其发展；倡导身教，践行不言之教，以自身行动示范影响他人，如家长、领导以身作则；追求无为境界，从自然规律汲取智慧，平和应对生活、工作，实现和谐统一。

The enlightenment of the chapter

When facing difficulties and tough opponents, use softness to overcome hardness and leverage flexibility. Gentle communication, for example, can seal negotiation deals. Recognize invisible power, value non-interference, and follow the laws. In child-rearing, granting freedom aids development. Set an example and practice wordless teaching, like parents and leaders do. Seek the non-interference realm, draw on nature's laws, and handle life and work calmly for harmonious unity.

第四十四章

míng yǔ shēn shú qīn shēn yǔ huò shú duō dé yǔ wáng shú bìng
名与身孰亲？身与货孰多？得与亡孰病？

shèn ài bì dà fèi duō cáng bì hòu wáng gù zhī zú bù rǔ zhī zhǐ bù dài kě yǐ cháng jiǔ
甚爱必大费，多藏必厚亡。故知足不辱[①]，知止不殆，可以长久。

注释

① 故知足不辱：通行本作“知足不辱”。此处按帛书本等校正，以体现上下句的因果关系。

今译

名誉和生命，哪个更亲近？生命与财富，哪个更重要？得到与失去，哪一个更有害？

过度贪爱，必有大耗费；聚敛太多，必有大损失。所以，懂得知足，就不会受辱；懂得适可而止，就不会遇险，这样才能长久。

英译

Which is dearer, fame or life? Which is more valuable, life or wealth? Which is more harmful, gain or loss?

Excessive love will bring great cost; excessive hoarding will lead to heavy loss. Therefore, he who knows contentment will not be disgraced; he who knows where to stop will not be in danger. Thus he can endure.

本章主旨

通过对比名誉、财富与生命的价值，批判过度追名逐利的行为，强调生命的珍贵，倡导人们懂得知足和适可而止，只有这样才能避免祸患，保持长久的平安与稳定。

The gist of the chapter

By comparing the value of fame, wealth and life, criticize the excessive pursuit of fame and fortune, emphasize the value of life, and advocate that people should know how to be content, believing that this can avoid dangers and maintain long-term peace and stability.

本章启示

要权衡名誉、生命、财富的轻重，明晰价值取向，重视自身健康与幸福；克制欲望，防止因过度贪恋名利财富而损耗精力、陷入险境；懂得知足知止，避免贪得无厌，以保持内心平静，实现长久安稳。

The enlightenment of the chapter

One should weigh the importance of fame, life, and wealth, clarify one's values, and attach importance to one's own health and well-being. Restrain desires to prevent depleting energy and getting into dangerous situations due to excessive greed for fame, fortune, and wealth. Understand the significance of contentment and knowing when to stop, avoid insatiable greed, maintain inner peace, and achieve long-term stability.

第四十五章

dà chéng ruò quē qí yòng bù bì dà yíng ruò chōng qí yòng bù qióng
大成若缺，其用不弊。大盈若冲，其用不穷。
dà zhí ruò qū dà qiǎo ruò zhuō dà biàn ruò nè
大直若屈，大巧若拙，大辩若讷。
zào shèng hán jìng shèng rè qīng jìng wéi tiān xià zhèng
躁胜寒，静胜热。清静为天下正。

今译

最圆满似缺损，作用却无失；最充盈若空虚，效用却无尽。最正直像弯曲，最灵巧如拙笨，最善辩似口讷。

躁动可驱寒，平静能耐热。清静无为才是天下的正道。

英译

Great perfection seems imperfect, yet its use is never impaired. Great fullness seems void, yet its use is never exhausted. Great straightness seems crooked. Great skill seems clumsy. Great eloquence seems inarticulate.

Activity overcomes cold; stillness overcomes heat. Tranquility and "wu-wei" (non-action) are the correct way for the world.

本章主旨

本章以"大成若缺"等表述阐述事物本质与表象之间的辩证关系，

强调透过现象看本质；借“静胜热”突出“静”的重要性，并由此延伸至修身与治世，主张以清静无为的方式实现个人修养的提升与社会的安定有序。

The gist of the chapter

This chapter incisively expounds the profound dialectical relationship between the essence and the outward appearance of things, employing vivid phrases such as “Great perfection seems imperfect”. Through these expressions, it deftly highlights how the true essence can be discerned beneath the surface phenomena, guiding us to look beyond mere appearances. Furthermore, by invoking the principle of “stillness overcoming heat”, it underscores the paramount significance of cultivating inner peace. This concept is then artfully extended to the realms of self-cultivation and governance. It advocates for the elevation of personal moral and spiritual cultivation, as well as the establishment and maintenance of social stability and order, all achieved through the practice of tranquility and non-interference. In so doing, it offers profound insights into both individual self-improvement and the harmonious operation of society.

本章启示

接纳事物的不完美，关注内在本质与实际价值，包容自身与他人缺点；即便成就斐然，也要保持谦逊、低调内敛，不断进取；不被表象迷惑，注重培养内在真实品质，如正直、灵巧、有辩才等；以平和心态处事，追求内心宁静，冷静应对外界，坚守自我以更好适应生活。

The enlightenment of the chapter

Embrace the imperfections of things, prioritize the inner essence and practical value, and tolerate personal and others’ flaws. Even with great achievements, stay humble, keep a low profile, and be reserved while pursuing continuous progress. Don't be misled by appearances; instead, focus on cultivating inner virtues like integrity, skill, and eloquence. Approach matters with a peaceful mind, seek inner tranquility, calmly face the external world, and stay true to yourself for a better adaptation to life.

第四十六章

tiān xià yǒu dào　què zǒu mǎ yǐ fèn　tiān xià wú dào　róng mǎ shēng
天下有道，却走马以粪。天下无道，戎马生
yú jiāo
于郊。

zuì mò dà yú duō yù　jiù mò dà yú yù dé　huò mò dà yú bù zhī zú　gù
罪莫大于多欲，咎莫大于欲得，祸莫大于不知足。① 故
zhī zú zhī zú　héng zú yǐ
知足之足，恒足矣。

注释

① 罪莫大于多欲，咎莫大于欲得，祸莫大于不知足：通行本作"祸莫大于不知足，咎莫大于欲得"；帛书本、竹简本分别作"罪莫大于可欲""罪莫厚于甚欲"。据安伦等校勘，采用竹简本的句序，与下文"故知足之足，恒足矣"衔接。

今译

治理天下合乎"道"，就可退还战马用于农耕；世道混乱无道，战马于战场郊外产驹。

最大的罪过是欲望过剩，最大的过失是贪得无厌，最大的灾祸是不知满足。所以，懂得知足并保持知足，才是长久的知足。

英译

When Dao prevails in the world, war-horses are sent back for farming. When Dao is lost in the world, war-horses foal on the battlefield outskirts.

There is no guilt greater than having excessive desire; there is no fault greater than being greedy; there is no misfortune greater than not knowing contentment. Therefore, the contentment of knowing contentment is a perpetual contentment.

本章主旨

本章通过对有道与无道时战马用途的对比表达反战思想，批判不知足与贪得无厌的欲望，强调知足才会获得长久的满足，倡导人们克制欲望、珍惜已有，以达内心平和与安宁。

The gist of the chapter

This chapter contrasts the use of war-horses in a well-ordered and chaotic world, with the former seeing them used for farming and the latter for war, thus expressing a strong anti-war sentiment. It also criticizes the vices of insatiability and excessive acquisitiveness, considering them as the root causes of misfortunes. The chapter advocates that "the contentment of knowing contentment is an enduring contentment", encouraging people to restrain their desires, cherish what they have, and attain inner peace and tranquility.

本章启示

倡导珍视和平，明白和谐稳定环境是发展基础，国家与个人都应维护；要克制欲望，警惕贪婪，因为不知足、贪得无厌易引发灾祸；学会知足，珍惜已有，以知足常乐心态追求内心宁静与富足，不被欲望左右。

The enlightenment of the chapter

It is advocated to cherish peace and understand that a harmonious and stable environment serves as the foundation for development. Both countries and individuals should strive to maintain it. One should restrain his desires and be vigilant against greed, for insatiability and avarice are likely to lead to disasters. Learn to be content with what one has, cherish the existing possessions, and pursue inner tranquility and richness with the mindset that contentment brings happiness, instead of being controlled by desires.

第四十七章

bù chū hù zhī tiān xià bù kūi yǒu jiàn tiān dào qí chū mí yuǎn qí zhī
不出户，知天下；不窥牖，见天道。其出弥远，其知
mí shǎo shì yǐ shèng rén bù xíng ér zhī bù jiàn ér míng bù wéi ér chéng
弥少。是以圣人不行而知，不见而明，不为而成。

今译

不出家门，便知天下事。不看窗外，亦知天道规律。外出越远，所知越浅。因此，圣人不出行能知事理，不亲见能明真相，不妄为能获成功。

英译

Without going out of doors, one can know the whole world; without looking out of the windows, one can perceive the Dao of Heaven. The further one goes out, the less one knows. Therefore, the sage knows without traveling, perceives without seeing, and accomplishes without acting rashly.

本章主旨

本章强调通过内省体悟而非向外追逐来认知天下事理与自然规律，批判盲目外求行为，阐述圣人依“道”而行、无为而治的境界，揭示了一种以内心体悟和把握“道”为主的独特认识论。

The gist of the chapter

This chapter emphasizes the importance of understanding the principles of the world and the laws of nature through introspection and contemplation rather than by blindly pursuing external things. It criticizes the behavior of seeking outwardly without due consideration, elaborates on the realm of sages who act in accordance with Dao and govern by "wu-wei" (non-action). It reveals a unique epistemology that focuses on comprehending and grasping Dao through inner experiences.

本章启示

重视内在思考，透过现象洞察本质规律，深度思考以解决复杂问题；避免盲目外求，获取外界信息后要回归本心反思消化，将知识内化为智慧；领悟无为智慧，顺应事物发展规律，因势利导促成目标，如教育与工作中顺势而为；培养宏观思维，超越局部细节，把握全局，做出前瞻性决策。

The enlightenment of the chapter

Give prominence to inner contemplation. See through surface phenomena to discern the fundamental laws, and engage in profound reflection to tackle intricate problems. Steer clear of mindlessly seeking answers from the outside world. Once external information is acquired, it is essential to retreat into inner reflection and assimilation, transforming knowledge into wisdom within. Grasp the essence of the wisdom of "wu-wei" (non-action), align with the developmental laws of things, and nimbly guide the situation to attain objectives as the circumstances demand. For instance, in the realms of education and work, one should act in harmony with the prevailing trends. Cultivate a macroscopic mindset, rise above petty details, have a firm grasp of the overall situation, and make insightful and forward-thinking decisions.

第四十八章

wéi xué rì yì wéi dào rì sǔn sǔn zhī yòu sǔn yǐ zhì yú wú wéi wú
为学日益，为道日损。损之又损，以至于无为。无
wéi ér wú bù wéi
为而无不为。

qǔ tiān xià héng yǐ wú shì jí qí yǒu shì bù zú yǐ qǔ tiān xià
取天下恒以无事。及其有事，不足以取天下。

今译

学习知识，一天比一天增加（知识）；修炼大道，一天比一天减少（欲念）。减少又减少，直至无为境地。达到无为的境地，反而无所不成。

治理天下，总是要清静无为。如果滋事妄为，就无法治理好天下。

英译

In the pursuit of learning, one's knowledge increases day by day. In the pursuit of Dao, one's desires are reduced day by day. Keep reducing until reaching the state of tranquility and "wu-wei" (non-action). In the state of tranquility and "wu-wei" (non-action), nothing can be unaccomplished.

To govern the world, one should always uphold the principle of tranquility and "wu-wei" (non-action). If there is excessive interference, the world cannot be governed well.

本章主旨

本章对比“为学”与“为道”的差异，指出“为道”须不断减损私欲杂念以达“无为”之境，强调“无为”能成就万事，进而将此理念延伸至治国理政，倡导统治者以不生事扰民来实现天下大治。

The gist of the chapter

This chapter contrasts the differences between “pursuing learning” and “pursuing Dao”, pointing out that “pursuing Dao” requires continuous reduction of selfish desires and distracting thoughts to reach the state of “wu-wei” (non-action). It emphasizes that through “wu-wei” (non-action), all things can be accomplished. Furthermore, this concept is extended to governance, advocating that rulers should avoid creating unnecessary troubles and disturbing the people, thus achieving the great governance of the world.

本章启示

平衡“为学”的知识积累与“为道”的心灵修养，兼顾能力提升与内心净化；追求“无为”境界，减少欲望执念，顺应自然规律行事；领悟“无为而无不为”智慧，放下对结果的执着，专注过程，自然收获成果；秉持“取天下以无事”理念，无论是社会治理还是团队合作，减少不必要干预，激发内在活力。

The enlightenment of the chapter

Balance the knowledge accumulation of “pursuing learning” and the spiritual cultivation of pursuing Dao, taking into account both the improvement of abilities and the purification of the mind. Pursue the realm of “wu-wei” (non-action), reduce desires and obsessions, and act in accordance with the laws of nature. Comprehend the wisdom of "nothing cannot be unaccomplished without interference", let go of attachment to results, focus on the process, and naturally reap the fruits. Adhere to the concept of "governing the world with non-interference". Whether in social governance or team cooperation, reduce unnecessary intervention and stimulate internal vitality.

第四十九章

shèng rén héng wú xīn yǐ bǎi xìng xīn wéi xīn shàn zhě wú shàn zhī
圣人恒无心①，以百姓心为心。善者，吾善之；
bù shàn zhě wú yì shàn zhī dé shàn xìn zhě wú xìn zhī bù xìn zhě wú
不善者，吾亦善之，德善。信者，吾信之；不信者，吾
yì xìn zhī dé xìn
亦信之，德信。

shèng rén zài tiān xià xī xī yān wèi tiān xià hún qí xīn bǎi xìng jiē zhù
圣人在天下，歙歙焉，为天下浑其心。百姓皆注
qí ěr mù shèng rén jiē hái zhī
其耳目，圣人皆孩之。

注释

① 恒无心：通行本作“无常心”，帛书乙本作“恒无心”。无心者，无私心也，是指圣人没有私心成见。而“无常心”则有心无所主的曲解，故据帛书乙本等予以校正。

今译

圣人常常没有私心，以百姓的心为自己的心。对于善良的人，我善待他；对于不善良的人，我也善待他，这样可使人人向善。对于守信的人，我信任他；对于不守信的人，我也信任他，这样可使人人守信。

圣人治理天下，会收敛自己的欲念，使天下人的心思归于浑朴。百姓们都专注于自己的耳目，圣人使他们都回到婴孩般纯朴的状态。

英译

The sage always has no concern of his own. He takes the concern of the people as his concern. For those who are good, I treat them with goodness; for those who are not good, I also treat them with goodness. Thus, true goodness is achieved. For those who are trustworthy, I trust them; for those who are not trustworthy, I also trust them. Thus, true trustworthiness is achieved.

The sage, when governing the world, always restrains himself and makes the people's minds simple and pure. The people all focus on their own ears and eyes, while the sage treats them all as children (while the sage leads them all back to the innocent and simple state of infants).

本章主旨

主张统治者应无私，以百姓之心为心，对百姓无论善恶、信与不信都予以善待和信任，通过收敛自身欲望，使百姓回归浑朴纯真状态，以达到社会和谐之目的。

The gist of the chapter

It is advocated that rulers should be selfless, taking the will of the people as their own. They should treat all people, whether good or bad, trustworthy or untrustworthy, with kindness and trust. By restraining their own desires, rulers can guide the people to return to a simple and innocent state, thus achieving the goal of social harmony.

本章启示

秉持以民为本，关注他人需求，站在对方立场思考，如管理者考虑员工利益；以包容之心待人，传递善与信任，用积极态度影响他人转变，如老师关爱调皮学生；自身保持平和，引导大众归真，在复杂外界中沉稳应对，以包容引导大众树立正观；放下偏见，平等对待众人，不因外在差异区别对待，促进社会和谐。

The enlightenment of the chapter

Adopt a people-oriented approach, focus on others' needs, and empathize. For instance, managers should prioritize employees' interests. Show inclusiveness, convey kindness and trust, and positively influence others to change, like teachers caring for mischievous students. Stay composed, guide the public towards simplicity and innocence, respond calmly to the complex world, and foster a correct outlook with an inclusive mindset. Set aside prejudices, treat all equally without discrimination based on external differences, and thus promote social harmony.

第五十章

chū shēng rù sǐ shēng zhī tú shí yǒu sān sǐ zhī tú shí yǒu sān rén zhī shēng shēng dòng zhī sǐ dì yì shí yǒu sān fú hé gù yǐ qí shēng shēng zhī hòu

出生入死，生之徒，十有三；死之徒，十有三；人之生生，动之死地，亦十有三。夫何故？以其生生之厚。

gài wén shàn shè shēng zhě lù xíng bù yù sì hǔ rù jūn bù pī jiǎ bīng sì wú suǒ tóu qí jiǎo hǔ wú suǒ cuò qí zhǎo bīng wú suǒ róng qí rèn fú hé gù yǐ qí wú sǐ dì

盖闻善摄生者，陆行不遇兕虎，入军不被甲兵。兕无所投其角，虎无所措其爪，兵无所容其刃。夫何故？以其无死地。

今译

人从生到死，长寿的占十分之三，短命的占十分之三，本想养生却因过度而为去世的也占十分之三。为何会这样呢？是因为他们为了求生而过度滋养自身。

据说善于护佑生命的人，在陆地行走碰不到犀牛和老虎，身处军队也不会为兵器所伤。对于这类人，犀牛的角无法顶到他，老虎的爪无法抓到他，士兵的兵器也刺不到他。这是为什么呢？因为他从不会让自己处于危险致命的境地。

英译

From birth to death, three-tenths live long lives, three-tenths die prematurely, and three-tenths try hard to stay alive but end up courting death. Why? Because they overdo efforts to preserve life.

It is said that those who are good at preserving life meet no rhinos or tigers on land, and are unharmed by armored soldiers in battlefields. Rhinos can't find where to thrust their horns, tigers can't find where to use their claws, and soldiers can't find where to stab their blades. Why is this so? It is because such people never put themselves in the realm of death (in a dangerous and life-threatening situation).

本章主旨

本章通过对长寿、短命及自促死亡三类人的分析，指出过度奉养有害生命，进而阐述善于养生之人能因顺应自然、不妄为而远离危险，体现了“无为”“少私寡欲”的养生理念及依“道”而行的思想。

The gist of the chapter

Through the analysis of three types of people: those with long lives, those with short lives, and those who hasten their own deaths, this chapter points out that excessive indulgence in overdoing health preservation is harmful to life. Furthermore, it expounds that those who are good at preserving life can stay away from dangers by conforming to nature and not acting recklessly. This reflects the ideas of "wu-wei" (non-action), "reducing selfishness and minimizing desires" in life-preserving, and acting in accordance with Dao.

本章启示

倡导适度生活，不过度贪恋物质享受，避免因纵欲损害健康与陷入困境，注重精神富足；主张顺应自然规律养生，保持良好生活习惯与平和心态，冷静应对困难；强调增强安全意识，提前防范各类风险，保护生命财产；重视关注内在精神，通过培养兴趣、学习等丰富内心，提升生命质量，从容面对生活。

The enlightenment of the chapter

Advocate a moderate lifestyle. Don't be overly obsessed with material enjoyment to avoid damaging your health and getting into trouble due to excessive indulgence. Instead, focus on spiritual richness. Propose following the laws of nature for health preservation, maintaining good living habits and a peaceful mindset, and calmly dealing with difficulties. Stress the need to enhance safety awareness, prevent various risks in advance, and protect life and property. Attach importance to paying attention to the inner spirit, enriching the heart through cultivating interests, learning, etc., improving the quality of life, and facing life with ease.

第五十一章

dào shēng zhī　dé xù zhī　wù xíng zhī　qì chéng zhī　shì yǐ wàn wù mò
道生之，德畜之，物形之，器成之[1]。是以万物莫
bù zūn dào ér guì dé　dào zhī zūn　dé zhī guì　fú mò zhī jué ér héng zì rán
不尊道而贵德。道之尊，德之贵，夫莫之爵而恒自然。
dào shēng zhī　dé xù zhī　zhǎng zhī yù zhī　chéng zhī shú zhī　yǎng zhī
道生之，德畜之，长之育之，成之熟之[2]，养之
fù zhī　shēng ér bù yǒu　wéi ér bù shì　zhǎng ér bù zǎi　shì wèi xuán dé
覆之；生而不有，为而不恃，长而不宰，是谓玄德。

注释

① 器成之：通行本作“势成之”，含义不清。帛书甲、乙本作“器成之”，语义连贯，符合万物经过道生、德蓄、成形、成器的连贯表述。

② 成之熟之：通行本作“亭之毒之”。据高亨等考证，“亭”“毒”分别与“成”“熟”音同，可通用，此处按河上公本作“成之熟之”。

今译

道生成万物，德养育万物。万物呈现出各种各样的形态，环境使万物成长起来。所以，万物没有不尊崇道而珍视德的。道之所以被尊崇，德之所以被珍视，是因为道生长万物而不加以干涉，德畜养万物而不加以主宰，都是顺其自然。

所以，道生长万物，德养育万物，使万物生长发育，使万物成长成熟，使万物受到滋养呵护。生长万物而不据为已有，作育万物而不自恃已能，长养万物而不加以主宰，这就叫玄妙的德。

英译

Dao creates all things, and De nurtures them. All things take on various forms, and the environment enables all things to grow. Therefore, there is nothing that does not venerate Dao and value De. The reason why Dao is venerated and De is valued is that Dao allows all things to grow without interference, and De nurtures all things without dominating them, all following the course of nature.

Therefore, Dao creates all things, and De nurtures them, enabling all things to grow and develop, to mature and ripen, and to be nourished and cared for. It creates all things without possessing them, promotes all things without relying its ability, and nurtures all things without exercising its dominance. This is called mystical De.

本章主旨

本章论述道生万物、德养万物的核心作用，强调道与德不占有、不自恃、不主宰的特性，借此倡导人们顺应自然，以无私无为的态度对待万物。

The gist of the chapter

This chapter expounds upon the pivotal functions of Dao in creating all things and of De in fostering them. It underscores the essence of Dao and De, highlighting that they neither lay claim to possession, nor boast of their contributions, nor exert domineering control. Through such principles, it advocates that individuals should harmoniously align with the rhythms of nature, embracing a selfless and non-interference approach in their interactions with all things.

本章启示

应尊重自然规律，万物依道而生、循德而长，人类行事须顺应此规律，如农业与生态领域；重视品德修养，让道德成为自然行为，以高尚品德赢得尊重，构建和谐关系；秉持无私奉献精神，不居功自傲，像教师、医生般全心付出，不求回报；处理事务时顺应规律，避免强行干预，无论是教育孩子还是管理企业，都要适度引导，激发其内在活力。

The enlightenment of the chapter

We should revere the laws of nature. All things originate from Dao and grow in line with De. Human activities must align with these laws, particularly in agriculture and ecology. Emphasize moral cultivation, making virtuous conduct second nature. Earn respect and foster harmonious relationships through noble virtues. Uphold the spirit of selfless dedication. Avoid conceit even upon achieving success. Like teachers and doctors, give wholeheartedly without expecting reciprocation. In handling matters, adhere to the laws and refrain from forced interference. Whether educating children or running an enterprise, offer appropriate guidance to ignite internal vitality.

第五十二章

tiān xià yǒu shǐ yǐ wéi tiān xià mǔ jì dé qí mǔ yǐ zhī qí zǐ jì zhī
天下有始，以为天下母。既得其母，以知其子。既知
qí zǐ fù shǒu qí mǔ mò shēn bù dài
其子，复守其母，没身不殆。

sè qí duì bì qí mén zhōng shēn bù qín kāi qí duì jǐ qí shì zhōng
塞其兑，闭其门，终身不勤。开其兑，济其事，终
shēn bù jiù
身不救。

jiàn xiǎo yuē míng shǒu róu yuē qiáng yòng qí guāng fù guī qí míng
见小曰明，守柔曰强。用其光，复归其明，
wú yí shēn yāng shì wéi xí cháng
无遗身殃，是为袭常。

今译

天下万物都有本始，这个本始可以作为天下万物的根源。既然知道了万物的根源，就能认识万物；既然认识了万物，又能持守着万物的根源，那么终身都不会有危险。

塞住欲念的孔穴，闭起欲念的门径，终身都不会有烦扰之事。如果打开欲念的孔穴，助长欲望之事，终身都不可救治。

能察见细微的叫作“明”，能持守柔弱的叫作“强”。运用外在的光芒，返照内在的澄明，不给自己带来灾殃，这就叫作沿袭恒常的道。

英译

There is the origin of the world, which can be regarded as the Mother of the world. Once one knows the Mother, he may know her children; once he knows her children, he may keep to the Mother, thus he will be free from danger all his life.

Block the vents of his sense organs, close the gates of desires, and he will be free from toil all his life. Open the vents of his sense organs, encourage the matters that fuel desires, and he will be beyond salvation all his life.

Perceiving the subtle is called enlightenment, keeping the soft is called power. Use its light and return to the bright, one may avoid bringing misfortune upon himself. This is called following the eternal Dao.

本章主旨

本章阐述万物有根源，认识根源可认识万物，进而提出要堵塞欲望之门以避烦扰，还强调察微守柔的重要性，倡导以智慧之光返照内心，以达常道、避灾祸。

The gist of the chapter

This chapter expounds that all things have their origins. By recognizing the origins, one can understand all things. Furthermore, it proposes that one should block the doorways of desires to avoid troubles. It also emphasizes the importance of perceiving the subtle and keeping the soft. It advocates using the light of wisdom to reflect within, so as to attain the eternal Dao and avoid disasters.

本章启示

面对复杂事物，探寻根源以把握本质，有助于正确决策；克制欲望，坚守内心宁静，不被外界诱惑、左右，过安稳生活；注重细节，洞察细微，以柔克刚，灵活应对人际交往与困难挑战；合理运用智慧，内敛不炫耀，用于自我提升与内在修行，规避风险。

The enlightenment of the chapter

When facing complex things, exploring the root causes to grasp the essence helps make correct decisions. Restrain desires, maintain inner peace, and do not be swayed by external temptations, so as to lead a stable life. Pay attention to details, be perceptive of the subtle, use the strategy of "the soft overcoming the hard", and flexibly deal with interpersonal relationships, difficulties and challenges. Reasonably apply wisdom, be reserved without showing off, and use it for self-improvement and inner cultivation to avoid risks.

第五十三章

shǐ wǒ jiè rán yǒu zhī xíng yú dà dào wéi yǐ shì wèi
使我介然有知，行于大道，唯迤是畏[1]。
dà dào shèn yí ér rén hào jìng cháo shèn chú tián shèn wú cāng
大道甚夷，而人[2]好径。朝甚除[3]，田甚芜，仓
shèn xū fú wén cǎi dài lì jiàn yàn yǐn shí cái huò yǒu yú shì wèi dào kuā
甚虚。服文彩，带利剑，厌饮食，财货有余，是谓盗夸。
fēi dào yě zāi
非道也哉。

注释

① 唯迤是畏：通行本作“唯施是畏”，“施”为“斜”“邪”，“施”可读为“迤”，两者音、义同，此处采用安伦等的校勘作“唯迤是畏”。

② 人：通行本作“民”，古代“民”“人”可通用，而此处“人”亦包含“人君”“统治者”之意。

③ 朝甚除：“除”有“整洁”“颓败”等不同的解读，此处采用马叙伦、陈鼓应等的释义。

今译

即使我稍有认识，在大道上行走，也唯恐走上邪路。

大道虽然平坦，但有人喜欢走邪路。朝政腐败已极，弄得农田荒芜，仓库十分空虚，而君主仍穿着锦绣的衣服，佩戴着锋利的宝剑，饱餐精美的食物，搜刮占有富余的财货，这就叫作强盗头子。这是多么无道啊！

英译

Even if I have little knowledge when walking on the the great way, I am afraid of straying onto the wrong path.

The great way is level, yet some people still prefer to take bypaths. The governance of the state is extremely corrupt, the farmlands lie waste and the granaries are extremely empty. However, the rulers still wear splendid brocade clothes, carry sharp swords, feast on delicious and exquisite food, and seize and hoard excessive wealth and goods. This is called the chief of robbers. How contrary to Dao!

本章主旨

以“行于大道，唯迤是畏”强调守道的重要性，借“朝甚除，田甚芜”等现象，批判统治者荒淫无道、穷奢极欲，揭示其行为的强盗本质，侧面表达老子希望统治者遵循大道、以民为本的政治主张。

The gist of the chapter

The statement “walking on the great way, one only fears deviating from it” emphasizes the importance of abiding by Dao. By citing phenomena such as “The governance of the state is extremely corrupt, the farmlands lie waste”, it criticizes rulers for their licentiousness and insatiable extravagance, and reveals the robbers-like nature of their actions. Indirectly, it expresses Laozi’s political proposition that rulers should follow the great Dao and take the people as the foundation.

本章启示

人生应坚守正道，勿因捷径诱惑而误入歧途，脚踏实地追求目标；无论是个人还是领导者，都要关注民生，摒弃追求表面浮华与个人享受的行为；崇尚俭朴生活，减少对物质的过度依赖，丰富精神世界；树立正确价值观，坚守道德底线，通过正当途径获取财富，不取不义之财。

The enlightenment of the chapter

In life, one should steadfastly adhere to the righteous path, remaining impervious to the allure of shortcuts that could lead to deviation, and pursue goals with a diligent and down-to-earth approach. Whether it is an individual or a leader, there should be a genuine focus on the people's well-being. Leaders, in particular, should eschew behaviors that prioritize superficial vanity and personal indulgence. It is advisable to advocate for a simple lifestyle, minimizing excessive reliance on material possessions, and instead, strive to enrich the spiritual realm. One should establish correct values, firmly hold fast to the moral baseline, acquire wealth through legitimate means, and under no circumstances seek ill-gotten gains.

第五十四章

shàn jiàn zhě bù bá shàn bào zhě bù tuō zǐ sūn yǐ jì sì bù chuò
善建者不拔，善抱者不脱，子孙以祭祀不辍。

xiū zhī yú shēn qí dé nǎi zhēn xiū zhī yú jiā qí dé nǎi yú xiū zhī yú
修之于身，其德乃真。修之于家，其德乃余。修之于

xiāng qí dé nǎi zhǎng xiū zhī yú guó qí dé nǎi fēng xiū zhī yú tiān xià
乡，其德乃长。修之于国[①]，其德乃丰。修之于天下，

qí dé nǎi pǔ
其德乃普。

gù yǐ shēn guān shēn yǐ jiā guān jiā yǐ xiāng guān xiāng yǐ guó guān
故以身观身，以家观家，以乡观乡，以国观

guó yǐ tiān xià guān tiān xià wú hé yǐ zhī tiān xià rán zāi yǐ cǐ
国，以天下观天下。吾何以知天下然哉？以此。

注释

① 国：竹简本、帛书甲本作“邦”，后人将“邦”改为“国”，主要是避汉高祖刘邦的名讳。通行本沿用“国”，更易理解和接受。

今译

善于建德的人，他的建树不可拔除。善于抱持大道的人，他的抱持不会脱落，这样子孙后代的祭祀就会世代相承，不会断绝。

以道修身，他的德就会纯真。以道修家，他的德就会充裕。以道修乡，他的德就会增长。以道修国，他的德就会丰足。以道修天下，他的德就会普及。

所以，要以修道之身观照他人之身，以修道之家观照其他家族，以

修道之乡观照其他乡里，以修道之国观照其他邦国，以修道之天下观照天下。我是怎么知道天下的情况就是这样的呢？就是依据这一方法。

英译

Those who are good at cultivating De establish something unshakable. Those who are good at embracing Dao hold it firmly, and thus from generation, to generation, their descendants will offer ancestral sacrifices without cease.

He who cultivates Dao with oneself, his De will be genuine. Cultivates Dao in the family, his De will be abundant. Cultivates Dao in the township, his De will multifly. Cultivates Dao in the state, his De will prosper. Cultivates Dao in the world, his De will be universal.

Therefore, observe the others with the cultivated himself; observe other families with the cultivated family; observe other townships with the cultivated township; observe other states with the cultivated state; observe the world with the cultivated world. How do I know this is so? By this.

本章主旨

本章借“善建”“善抱”喻“道”之稳固持久，阐述“德”由修身至齐家、治国、平天下的推广价值，提出从个体到天下各层面的观察认知方法，指明对“道”“德”的体悟运用是认识世界的依据。

The gist of the chapter

Using the metaphors of “being good at establishing De” and “being good at embracing Dao” to illustrate the stability and endurance of Dao, this chapter expounds on the value of De in its extension from self-cultivation to family harmony, state governance, and bringing peace to the world. It proposes methods of observation and understanding at various levels, from the individual to the entire world. It also points out that the comprehension and application of Dao and De serve as the basis for understanding the world.

本章启示

本章强调修身是个人与社会和谐的起点，通过内在修养，逐步影响家庭、国家乃至天下。它提醒我们，真正的治理应从自身开始，通过内在修养，顺应自然，以德服人，实现个人与社会的和谐。治国平天下的关键在于领导者以身作则，遵循“道”的原则，无为而治。

The enlightenment of the chapter

This chapter emphasizes that self-cultivation is the starting point for the harmony between individuals and society. Through inner cultivation, one can gradually influence the family, the country, and even the whole world. It reminds us that true governance should begin with oneself. Only by cultivating oneself internally, conforming to nature, and winning people over with virtue can we achieve harmony between individuals and society. The key to governing the country and bringing peace to the world lies in leaders setting an example and following the principles of Dao to practice governance through non-interference.

第五十五章

hán dé zhī hòu zhě bǐ rú chì zǐ fēng chài huī shé bù shì jué niǎo měng
含德之厚者，比如赤子。蜂虿虺蛇不螫①，攫鸟猛
shòu bù bó gǔ ruò jīn róu ér wò gù wèi zhī pìn mǔ zhī hé ér zuī zuò jīng zhī
兽不博②，骨弱筋柔而握固。未知牝牡之合而朘作，精之
zhì yě zhōng rì háo ér bù shà hé zhī zhì yě
至也；终日号而不嗄，和之至也。

hé yuē cháng zhī cháng yuē míng yì shēng yuē xiáng xīn shǐ qì yuē
和曰常③，知常曰明。益生曰祥，心使气曰
qiáng wù zhuàng zé lǎo shì wèi bù dào bù dào zǎo yǐ
强。物壮则老，是谓不道，不道早已。

注释

① 蜂虿虺蛇不螫：河上公本等作“毒虫不螫”，此处按王弼本、帛书本等的表述。

② 攫鸟猛兽不博：王弼本作“猛兽不据，攫鸟不博”，此处按竹简本、帛书本等的表述。

③ 和曰常：通行本作“知和曰常”，而帛书本、竹简本均无“知”字，据此校正。

今译

道德涵养深厚的人，就好比初生的婴孩。蜂蝎毒蛇不螫咬他，凶禽猛兽不攻击他。他的筋骨柔弱，但拳头握得紧而有力。他虽然不知道男女交合之事，但他的小生殖器却常常勃起，这是因为精气充沛的缘故。他整天啼哭，但嗓子不会沙哑，这是因为气和谐至极的缘故。

和谐叫作“常”(恒常法则),知道“常”叫作“明”。纵欲贪生就会遭殃,欲念主使精气就叫作逞强。事物过于壮盛了就会变衰老,这就叫不合于道,不守常道就会很快死亡。

英译

One who is rich in De is like a newborn baby. Wasps, scorpions, and poisonous snakes won't sting or bite him; predatory birds and fierce beasts will not attack him. His bones are weak and sinews soft, yet his grip is firm. Innocent of sexual matters, yet he can have his penile erection due to full vital essence. He can cry all day without getting hoarse due to perfect internal harmony.

Harmony is called the constant law. To know the constant law is enlightenment. To seek excessive life pleasure is ominous. To rule essence by desire is bravado. Things decline when overly strong as it goes against Dao, and what goes against Dao will perish soon.

本章主旨

本章借婴儿自然状态推崇纯真质朴,以其精气充沛、和气纯厚喻道德深厚之态;指出认识淳和之理为“常”,知“常”为“明”;警示贪生纵欲、心使气为逞强不祥;强调事物壮极则衰,不合道易早亡,凸显遵道守常的重要性。

The gist of the chapter

This chapter praises purity and simplicity through the natural state of an infant. The infant's rich essence-qi and pure harmonious qi symbolize a high level of De. It states that grasping the principle of simplicity and harmony is "the constant law", and understanding this law is "enlightenment". It cautions that overindulgence in worldly pleasures and desires and forcing qi with the mind are acts of bravado and bring bad luck. It stresses that when things peak, they decline, and what goes against Dao is likely to perish early, underlining the significance of following Dao and abiding by the constant law.

本章启示

以赤子为榜样，保持纯真质朴，不被世俗污染；顺应自然规律，涵养精气，维持身心和谐；认识并遵循事物的和谐常理，克制欲望，理性平和应对生活；警惕盛极而衰，在强盛时坚守正道，保持谦虚谨慎，确保长久发展。

The enlightenment of the chapter

Taking infants as an example, one should stay innocent and simple, free from the taint of the secular world. Abide by the laws of nature, nurture vital energy, and keep the body and mind in harmony. Recognize and follow the harmonious principles of things, rein in desires, and respond to life rationally and tranquilly. Be wary of the decline that follows reaching the peak. In a prosperous situation, stick to the right path, stay modest and prudent to ensure sustained development.

第五十六章

zhī zhě bù yán yán zhě bù zhī
知者不言，言者不知。[①]

sè qí duì bì qí mén cuò qí ruì jiě qí fēn hé qí guāng tóng qí chén shì wèi xuán tóng
塞其兑，闭其门，挫其锐，解其纷，和其光，同其尘，是谓玄同。

gù bù kě dé ér qīn bù kě dé ér shū bù kě dé ér lì bù kě dé ér hài bù kě dé ér guì bù kě dé ér jiàn gù wèi tiān xià guì
故不可得而亲，不可得而疏；不可得而利，不可得而害；不可得而贵，不可得而贱。故为天下贵。

注释

① 知者不言，言者不知：据陈鼓应等校勘，“知者”疑作“智者”，此处将“知”解释为“智慧”。也有注本将其解释为“知道的人不说，说的人不知道”。

今译

有智慧的人不会夸夸其谈，那些夸夸其谈的不是有智慧的人。塞住嗜欲的孔窍，关闭嗜欲的门径；磨去锋利，消解纷争，调和光芒，混同尘世，这就叫作“玄同”。

达到这种“玄同”境界的人，人们无法与他亲近，也无法与他疏远；无法让他获利，也无法让他受害；无法使他高贵，也无法使他低贱，所以这样的人被天下人尊重。

英译

He who is wise does not speak, and he who speaks is not wise.

Block the openings of the sense organs, close the door of desires, blunt the sharp edges, untangle the entanglements, soften the glow, and blend with the secular world. This is what is called "mystical unity".

In this realm, one can't be befriended or alienated, benefited or harmed, exalted or humbled. Thus, he is honored by all under Heaven.

本章主旨

本章以"玄同"为核心，批判世俗智巧，倡导超越亲疏、利害、贵贱等世俗分别，达与道合一之境，体现道的超越性，同时蕴含无为而治的政治理念，强调其对个人精神自由与社会和谐稳定的意义。

The gist of the chapter

Centering on the notion of "mystical unity", this chapter condemns worldly cleverness and shrewdness. It advocates transcending worldly oppositions like intimacy and estrangement, advantages and disadvantages, nobility and humility, thus attaining a state of oneness with Dao. This mirrors the transcendence of Dao.

Simultaneously, it subtly conveys the political idea of governing through non-interference. It underscores the profound significance of this concept for both personal spiritual liberation and the harmonious stability of society.

本章启示

谨言慎行，用行动代替空谈，避免因言语而暴露浅薄，避免无端麻烦；克制欲望，减少对外界过度索求，保持内心平和，专注要事；韬光养晦，不露锋芒，以谦逊态度与人和谐共处，营造良好人际关系与团队氛围；超越亲疏利害，秉持平等公正原则处理事务与人际关系，赢得尊重、信任，促进和谐发展。

The enlightenment of the chapter

Be cautious in speeches and actions, replace empty talk with deeds, avoid exposing your shallowness through words, and prevent unnecessary troubles. Restrain your desires, reduce excessive pursuit of the outside world, maintain inner peace, and focus on important matters. Hide one's capabilities and bide one's time, do not show off one's abilities, get along harmoniously with others with a humble attitude, and create a good interpersonal and team atmosphere. Transcend personal relationships and self-interests, handle affairs and interpersonal relationships in accordance with the principles of equality and fairness, win respect and trust, and promote harmonious development.

第五十七章

yǐ zhèng zhì guó yǐ qí yòng bīng yǐ wú shì qǔ tiān xià wú hé yǐ zhī qí
以正治国，以奇用兵，以无事取天下。吾何以知其
rán zāi yǐ cǐ tiān xià duō jì huì ér mín mí pín mín duō lì qì guó jiā zī
然哉？以此：天下多忌讳，而民弥贫；民多利器，国家滋
hūn rén duō jì qiǎo qí wù zī qǐ fǎ lìng zī zhāng dào zéi duō yǒu
昏；人多伎巧，奇物滋起；法令滋彰，盗贼多有。

gù shèng rén yún wǒ wú wéi ér mín zì huà wǒ hào jìng ér mín zì
故圣人云：我无为而民自化，我好静而民自
zhèng wǒ wú shì ér mín zì fù wǒ wú yù ér mín zì pǔ
正，我无事而民自富，我无欲而民自朴。

qí zhèng mèn mèn qí mín chún chún qí zhèng chá chá qí mín quē
其政闷闷，其民淳淳。其政察察，其民缺
quē shì yǐ shèng rén fāng ér bù gē lián ér bù guì zhí ér bù sì guāng ér
缺。是以圣人方而不割，廉而不刿[1]，直而不肆，光而
bù yào
不耀。[2]

注释

① 廉而不刿：此处将其解释为“锐利而不伤人”。据陈鼓应等考证：“廉”，利；“刿”，伤。也有注本将“廉”解释为“廉洁”等。

② 通行本“其政闷闷，其民淳淳。其政察察，其民缺缺”及“是以圣人方而不割，廉而不刿，直而不肆，光而不耀”原在第五十八章的段前和段末位置，但与第五十八章内容在语义和逻辑上不相关联，据安伦等校勘，将其一并调整至本章，则语义连贯，逻辑严密。

今译

用清静无为的正道治理国家，用奇巧诡秘的谋略用兵，用不搅扰百姓的方式治理天下。我怎么知道是这样的呢？根据就在于：天下的禁忌越多，百姓就越贫穷；百姓的利器越多，国家就越混乱；人们的技巧越多，邪风怪事就越兴起；法令越是森严，盗贼反而就越多。

所以圣人说："我无作为，百姓就自然教化；我好清静，百姓就自然纯正；我不生事，百姓就自然富足；我无私欲，百姓就自然淳朴。"

政治宽厚，人民就淳朴；政治严苛，人民就狡黠。因此，有道的人方正而不割人，锐利而不伤人，直率而不放肆，光亮而不刺眼。

英译

To govern a state, uphold rectitude. In war, employ clever surprise tactics. To win the world, do nothing purposely. How do I know it is so? By the following facts: The more prohibitions there are, the poorer the people become. The more sharp weapons the people have, the greater disorder the state descends into. The more acts of craftiness the people perform, the more bizarre things appear. The more statutes and decrees there are, the more thieves and robbers emerge.

Therefore the sage says: "I have no contrived pursuits, and the people are transformed by themselves. I cherish stillness, and the people become upright by themselves. I do nothing purposely, and the people grow rich by themselves. I have no desires, and the people stay simple and honest by themselves."

When governance is dull and inactive, the people are simple and honest. When it's overly scrutinizing, they misbehave. Thus, the sages are square without cutting, sharp without wounding, straightforward without being unrestrained, bright without dazzling.

本章主旨

本章提出“以正治国，以奇用兵，以无事取天下”的理念，批判因过多禁令、权谋智巧、严苛法令等导致的社会乱象，倡导统治者无为而治，减少对百姓的干预，以实现返璞归真的社会风气，使百姓自然实现化育、端正、富足和淳朴。有道之人应遵循方正不伤人、锐利不刺人、直率不放肆、光亮不刺眼的行为准则，体现适度、和谐的处世哲学。

The gist of the chapter

This chapter puts forward the concept of “To govern a state, uphold rectitude. In war, employ clever surprise tactics. To win the world, do nothing purposely.” It criticizes the social chaos caused by excessive prohibitions, political maneuvers, and harsh laws. It advocates that rulers should govern by doing nothing purposely and reduce their interference with the people, so as to restore a simple and natural social governance, enabling the people to naturally achieve self-cultivation, rectitude, prosperity, and simplicity. Moreover, it points out that those who abide by Dao should follow the code of conduct of being upright without cutting others, sharp without hurting others, straightforward without being unrestrained, and bright without being dazzling, embodying a moderate and harmonious philosophy of life.

本章启示

治国要秉持正道，确保政策公正稳定，为社会发展筑牢根基；用兵或竞争时须灵活出奇，以创新策略克敌制胜；治理应减少对民众的不必要干预，给予其自由空间，激发其创造力，推动经济与社会发展；政策制定者要反思监管，避免过度限制；治国理政应宽松包容，激发民众淳朴本性；为人处世把握适度原则，品德、行为与才能展现不过度，避免极端。

The enlightenment of the chapter

When governing a country, one should adhere to the right path, ensure that policies are fair and stable, and lay a solid foundation for social development. When waging war or competing, one needs to be flexible and come up with unconventional strategies to defeat the enemy with innovative approaches. In governance, unnecessary interference with the people should be reduced, and they should be given free space to stimulate their creativity, thus promoting economic and social development. Policy-makers should reflect on supervision to avoid excessive restrictions. Governance should be lenient and inclusive to stimulate the people's simple nature. When dealing with people and things, one should grasp the principle of moderation. The demonstration of virtues, behaviors, and talents should not be excessive to avoid extremes.

第五十八章

huò xī fú zhī suǒ yǐ fú xī huò zhī suǒ fú shú zhī qí jí qí wú zhèng
祸兮福之所倚，福兮祸之所伏。孰知其极？其无正
yě zhèng fù wéi qí shàn fù wéi yāo rén zhī mí qí rì gù jiǔ
也。正复为奇，善复为妖。人之迷，其日固久。①

注释

① 如前章所述，本章原有的“其政闷闷，其民淳淳。其政察察，其民缺缺”与“是以圣人方而不割，廉而不刿，直而不肆，光而不耀”一并被调整至第五十七章。

今译

灾祸啊，幸福倚傍在它里面；幸福啊，灾祸藏伏在它之中。谁知道它们的究竟？这实在没有一个定准！正忽而变为邪，善忽而变为恶。人们对此的迷惑已经有长久的时日了。

英译

Misfortune is where fortune leans upon, and fortune is where misfortune lurks. Who knows their limits? There is no fixed standard. What is the normal turns into the abnormal, and what is the good turns into the evil. People have been bewildered for a long time.

本章主旨

本章强调祸福相互依存、相互转化且变化无常，提醒人们以平和心态看待。

The gist of the chapter

This chapter emphasizes that misfortune and fortune are interdependent, mutually transformative, and unpredictable, reminding people to view them with an even-tempered mindset.

本章启示

本章提醒我们在生活中要以辩证的思维看待事物，无论是面对成功还是失败，顺境还是逆境，都要保持平常心。当身处福境时，不能得意忘形，要警惕潜在的危机；当遭遇祸患时，也不要一蹶不振，要看到其中蕴含的转机。比如，一次工作上的挫折可能促使我们反思自身不足，从而提升能力，为未来的成功奠定基础；一时的成功如果让人骄傲自满，可能会引发后续的失败。

The enlightenment of the chapter

This chapter urges us to adopt a dialectical view in life: stay calm and balanced in success or failure, prosperity or adversity. In good times, beware of crises instead of being complacent. In bad times, find hidden turning points rather than being overwhelmed. For instance, work setbacks can spur self-reflection and growth, while arrogance from temporary success may bring future failures.

第五十九章

zhì rén shì tiān mò ruò sè fú wéi sè shì yǐ zǎo fú zǎo fú shì wèi
治人事天①，莫若啬②。夫唯啬，是以早服。早服是谓
chóng jī dé chóng jī dé zé wú bù kè wú bù kè zé mò zhī qí jí mò zhī
重积德，重积德则无不克，无不克则莫知其极，莫知
qí jí kě yǐ yǒu guó yǒu guó zhī mǔ kě yǐ cháng jiǔ shì wèi shēn gēn gù dǐ
其极可以有国，有国之母可以长久。是谓深根固柢，
cháng shēng jiǔ shì zhī dào
长生久视之道。

注释

① 事天：此处解释为“侍奉上天”，也有注本将其理解为“保养天赋”。

② 啬：此处解释为“节俭，爱惜资源”。

今译

治理百姓和侍奉上天，没有比珍惜资源更重要的了。正因为珍惜资源，才可以说是尽早服从天道；尽早服从天道，就是不断地积累德；不断地积累德，就没有什么不能攻克的；没有什么不能攻克，就没有人能知道他力量的极限；没有人能知道他力量的极限，他就可以担负起治理国家的重任。掌握了治理国家的根本原则，就可以使国家长治久安。这就叫作根深蒂固的长久之道。

英译

In governing people and serving Heaven, nothing is better than frugality. Only by being frugal can one submit to Dao early. Submitting to Dao early is called the accumulation of De. The accumulation of De enables one to overcome everything. Being able to overcome everything means that no one knows his limit. When no one knows his limit, he can govern a state. Grasping the fundamental principle of governing a state enables the governance to last long. This is called the way of deepening the roots, strengthening the foundation, and achieving everlasting existence.

本章主旨

本章提出“啬”是治人事天的关键，强调“啬”意味着早做准备与积累德，积累德能增强力量，使人可担当治国重任，最终实现国家长治久安，突出“啬”在个人修养与国家治理中的重要意义。

The gist of the chapter

It is proposed in this chapter that “frugality” is crucial for governing people and serving Heaven. It highlights that “frugality” entails early preparations and the accumulation of De, which strengthens one's power, enabling them to take on the heavy task of state governance and ultimately ensuring long-term state stability and security, thus underscoring the great significance of “frugality” in both personal cultivation and national governance.

本章启示

倡导节俭，在国家治理与个人生活中珍惜资源，避免浪费；提前储备资源、能力与品德，防患于未然，从容应对挑战；注重积累，无论是个人成长还是国家发展，厚积方能薄发；稳固根基，避免急功近利，以谋求长远发展；学会自我约束，克制欲望，自律生活，掌控人生，走向成功。

The enlightenment of the chapter

In national governance and personal life, advocate frugality, cherish resources and eschew waste. Pre-emptively reserve resources, capabilities and virtues to fend off potential issues and face challenges with composure. For both personal growth and national development, emphasize accumulation, only solid accumulation enables full potential realization. Stabilize the foundation, eschew eagerness for quick results, and pursue long-term development. Practice self-restraint, rein in desires, live a disciplined life, master your destiny, and progress towards success.

第六十章

zhì dà guó ruò pēng xiǎo xiān
治大国，若烹小鲜。

yǐ dào lì tiān xià qí guǐ bù shén fēi qí guǐ bù shén qí shén bù shāng
以道莅天下，其鬼不神。非其鬼不神，其神不伤

rén fēi qí shén bù shāng rén shèng rén yì bù shāng rén fú liǎng bù xiāng
人。非其神不伤人，圣人亦不伤人。夫两不相

shāng gù dé jiāo guī yān
伤，故德交归焉。

今译

治理大国，就像煎烹小鱼。用道来治理天下，那些鬼怪就不灵了。不仅鬼怪不灵了，神祇也不会伤害人。不仅神祇不伤害人，圣人也不会伤害人。鬼神和圣人都不伤害人，德行会自然归于天下众人。

英译

Governing a large state is like cooking a small fish. When one governs the world with Dao, the ghosts will lose their power. It's not that the ghosts lose power, but they cease to harm people. Not only they cease to harm people, but the sages also won't harm people. With neither of them harming people, De will thus return to the world.

本章主旨

本章以“烹小鲜”比喻治国，主张治国应遵循自然无为的“道”，

并指出以“道”治天下能使鬼怪、神灵不伤人，圣人亦不伤人，从而让德行自然遍布天下，实现社会和谐安定。

The gist of the chapter

Using “cooking a small fish” as a metaphor for state governance, this chapter advocates following Dao of naturalness and “wu-wei” (non-action). It also indicates that governing the world by Dao can prevent the ghosts, the spirits, and the sages from harming the people. Thus, De will spread naturally, bringing about social harmony and stability.

本章启示

治理国家要遵循规律，不过度干预，秉持无为而治理念，激发社会活力；以“道”治国，营造各方和谐共处的良好环境；执政者须敬畏权力，谨慎决策与行事，避免滥用权力；追求国家各方面发展的平衡，确保稳定与可持续发展。

The enlightenment of the chapter

When governing a state, one should follow the laws, refrain from excessive intervention, uphold the concept of governing by non-interference, and stimulate social vitality. Govern the country in accordance with Dao to create a favorable environment where all parties coexist harmoniously. Rulers should have a sense of awe for power, make decisions and act cautiously, and avoid the abuse of power. Pursue a balance in all aspects of national development to ensure stability and sustainable development.

第六十一章

dà guó zhě xià liú tiān xià zhī jiāo tiān xià zhī pìn pìn héng yǐ jìng
大 国[1] 者 下 流，天 下 之 交，天 下 之 牝[2]。牝 恒 以 静
shèng mǔ yǐ jìng wéi xià gù dà guó yǐ xià xiǎo guó zé qǔ xiǎo guó xiǎo guó
胜 牡，以 静 为 下。故 大 国 以 下 小 国，则 取 小 国；小 国
yǐ xià dà guó zé qǔ yú dà guó gù huò xià yǐ qǔ huò xià ér qǔ
以 下 大 国，则 取 于 大 国[3]。故 或 下 以 取，或 下 而 取。

dà guó bù guò yù jiān xù rén xiǎo guó bù guò yù rù shì rén fú liǎng zhě
大 国 不 过 欲 兼 畜 人，小 国 不 过 欲 入 事 人。夫 两 者
gè dé qí suǒ yù dà zhě yí wéi xià
各 得 其 所 欲，大 者 宜 为 下。

注释

① 国：帛书甲本作“邦”，后人将“邦”改为“国”，主要是避汉高祖刘邦的名讳。通行本沿用“国”，更易理解和接受。

② 天下之交，天下之牝：帛书甲本作“天下之牝，天下之交也”。此处采用通行本等的表述。

③ 则取于大国：通行本作“则取大国”，而“取于大国”是被动句式，意思是“被大国接纳”，故据帛书本校正。

今译

大国要像居于江河的下游那样，是天下交汇的地方，处于天下雌牝的位置。雌牝常凭借静柔战胜雄强，就是因为静柔处于低下的位置。所以，大国对小国谦下，就能使小国归附；小国对大国谦下，就能被大国接纳。因此，有的以谦下使他人归附，有的则以谦下被他人接纳。

大国不过是想网罗畜养小国，小国不过是想投靠归附大国。这样二者都能实现各自的愿望，而大国尤其应当谦下。

英译

A large state is like the lower reaches of a river: the junction of the world, or the feminine of the world. The feminine always conquers the masculine by her stillness, for stillness is considered a sort of a basement. Therefore, if a large state abases itself to a small state, it will win over a small state; and if a small state abases itself to a large state, it will be accepted by a large state. Thus some abase themselves to win over others, while some abase themselves to be accepted by others.

What a large state wants is to win over and shelter others, and what a small state wants is to be accepted and serve others. Thus, each gets what it wants, but a large state should especially abase itself.

本章主旨

本章以“大国者下流”阐述大国应谦下以得小国信赖，借“牝常以静胜牡”说明柔能克刚，指出大国、小国各有诉求，双方谦下才能各遂所愿、实现共赢，体现出对国家关系及利益平衡的思考。

The gist of the chapter

Using the metaphor of “a large state as the lower reaches”, this chapter advocates that large states should be humble to gain small states' trust. Citing “the feminine conquers the masculine by stillness” illustrates softness overcoming hardness. It notes that large and small states have distinct needs, and only through mutual humility can they meet their desires and achieve a win-win, reflecting insights on inter-state relations and interest balance.

本章启示

处于优势地位者，如大国或组织中的强者，应谦逊处下，赢得尊重与信任；面对强大对手，可采用以柔克刚的策略，灵活应变求发展；各类交往须相互尊重，考虑对方利益，实现互利共赢；实力强大、影响力大者，要承担更多责任，维护整体秩序与发展。

The enlightenment of the chapter

Those in dominant positions, like major countries or powerful entities in organizations, should be humble to gain respect and trust. When facing tough rivals, adopt a soft-over-hard strategy and adapt flexibly for development. In all interactions, mutual respect matters; consider others' interests for mutual benefit and win-win outcomes. The powerful should shoulder more responsibilities to ensure overall order and growth.

第六十二章

dào zhě wàn wù zhī ào shàn rén zhī bǎo bù shàn rén zhī suǒ bǎo měi yán
道者万物之奥，善人之宝，不善人之所保。美言
kě yǐ shì zūn měi xíng kě yǐ jiā rén rén zhī bù shàn hé qì zhī yǒu gù lì
可以市尊，美行可以加人①，人之不善，何弃之有。故立
tiān zǐ zhì sān gōng suī yǒu gǒng bì yǐ xiān sì mǎ bù rú zuò jìn cǐ dào
天子，置三公，虽有拱璧以先驷马，不如坐进此道。
gǔ rén zhī suǒ yǐ guì cǐ dào zhě hé bù yuē qiú yǐ dé yǒu zuì yǐ miǎn
古人之所以贵此道者何？不曰求以得②，有罪以免
yé gù wéi tiān xià guì
邪？故为天下贵。

注释

① 美言可以市尊，美行可以加人：通行本等作“美言可以市，尊行可以加人”，句型和押韵似有缺陷，此处按安伦等的校勘予以校正。

② 求以得：王弼本作“以求得”。“求以得”与“有罪以免”相对成文，此处按景龙碑本、傅奕本、帛书本等予以校正。

今译

道，是万物的奥妙之所在，是善人的法宝，也是不善人所应保持的。优美的言辞可以赢得尊敬，高尚的行为可以赢得尊重。即使是不善之人，又何必抛弃道呢？所以，设立天子，安排三公官员，即使有拱璧在先、驷马在后这样隆重的礼仪，还不如敬献给他们道。

古人之所以尊崇道，不就是有求可以得到，有罪过能够免除吗？如此，道才被天下人尊崇。

英译

Dao is the mystery of all things. It is the treasure of the good people, and those who are not good should also keep it. Fine words can win honor; good deeds can gain respect. Even those are not good, why should they abandon Dao? Hence, when the Son of Heaven is enthroned and the three ministers are appointed, even if there were grand tributes like presenting a large jade before four-horse chariots, it would be better to sit and present this Dao instead.

Why did the ancients value this Dao so much? Isn't it because the people can obtain what they seek and have their sins pardoned? Therefore, it is the most precious thing in the world.

本章主旨

本章阐述道是万物奥秘所在，对善恶之人都有价值，是珍贵宝物与依靠庇护。本章强调道的价值远超财物，因其能让人求愿得偿、罪过可免，所以为天下人所珍视。

The gist of the chapter

This chapter expounds that Dao is the mystery of all things, valuable to both the good and the bad as a precious treasure and a source of support and protection. It highlights that Dao's value surpasses material wealth, enabling people to fulfill wishes and be forgiven of sins, thus being highly prized in the world.

本章启示

道是万物根本，应重视对道的追求；善良有强大力量，要秉持善念；以包容之心对待不善之人，助其改过；注重言行，用美言美行赢得尊重、影响他人；摒弃虚荣，追求道的本质价值；敬畏道的力量，遵循规律，规范自身行为。

The enlightenment of the chapter

Dao is the essence of all things, deserving our earnest pursuit. Kindness is potent, so we should stay true to good intentions. Be inclusive of the unkind to aid their self-improvement. Mind our words and deeds, using kind speech and good acts to earn respect and sway others. Forsake vanity and seek the core value of Dao. Acknowledge Dao's power, abide by its principles, and regulate our conduct.

第六十三章

wéi wú wéi shì wú shì wèi wú wèi dà xiǎo duō shǎo bào yuàn yǐ dé
为无为，事无事，味无味。大小多少，报怨以德。

tú nán yú qí yì wéi dà yú qí xì tiān xià nán shì bì zuò yú yì tiān xià dà shì bì zuò yú xì shì yǐ shèng rén zhōng bù wéi dà gù néng chéng qí dà
图难于其易，为大于其细。天下难事，必作于易；天下大事，必作于细。是以圣人终不为大，故能成其大。

fú qīng nuò bì guǎ xìn duō yì bì duō nán shì yǐ shèng rén yóu nán zhī gù zhōng wú nán yǐ
夫轻诺必寡信，多易必多难。是以圣人犹难之，故终无难矣。

今译

以无为的态度去有所作为，以不滋事的方式去处理事务，将恬淡无味当作有味。以小为大，以少为多，以德行回报怨恨。

解决难题要从容易的地方入手，成就大事要从细微处做起。天下的难事，一定是由易事积累而成的；天下的大事，必定是从细小处做起。因此，圣人从不刻意追求做大事，反而能成就大业。

轻易允诺必然缺乏信用，看事情太过容易一定会遇到更多困难。所以，圣人总是把事情看得很难，因此最终没有难事。

英译

Accomplish without doing purposely; act without contrivances;

savor without flavors. Make the small big; make the few many; repay resentment with virtue.

Deal with the difficult while it is still easy; work on the great while it is still small. Difficult things under Heaven must start from the easy; great undertakings under Heaven must start from the small. Therefore, the sages never attempt to be great, and yet are able to accomplish greatness.

Those who lightly make promises are sure to lack faithfulness; those who think everything is easy are sure to encounter many difficulties. Therefore, the sages treat things as difficult, and thus never meet with difficulties.

本章主旨

本章倡导以无为、无事、无味的原则行事，秉持以德报怨理念；揭示解决难题须从易处着手、成就大事要从小事做起；强调不可轻诺，应重视困难，始终谨慎对待事务，以达成目标。

The gist of the chapter

This chapter advocates the principle of accomplishing without doing purposely, acting without contrivances, savoring without flavors, and repaying resentment with virtue. It shows that solving tough problems starts with the easy, and great achievements begin with small deeds. Stress against making hasty promises, taking difficulties seriously, and approaching all matters with caution for goal attainment.

本章启示

在行为处事方面，倡导无为而治，顺应规律，不过度干预；强调化繁为简，从易处、细微处着手解决难题、成就大事。在品德修养方面，主张以德报怨，用宽容德行化解矛盾；劝诫不贪大功，脚踏实地，专注于积累。在言行规范方面，提醒言出必行，不轻易许诺，承诺必践行以保诚信；还强调重视困难，充分预估、准备，避免轻视致难。

The enlightenment of the chapter

In behavior and dealing with matters: Advocate governing by non-interference, conform to the laws and avoid excessive interference. Simplify the complex, solve difficult problems, and achieve great things starting from the easy and subtle aspects. In moral cultivation: Advocate repaying resentment with virtue, resolve conflicts with tolerance, and admonish against craving for great achievements, focusing instead on down-to-earth accumulation. In words and deeds: Remind people to match their words with their deeds, without making promises lightly, and keep their promises to maintain integrity. And emphasize taking difficulties seriously, making full predictions and preparations to prevent difficulties arising from underestimation.

第六十四章

qí ān yì chí qí wèi zhào yì móu qí cuì yì pàn qí wēi yì sàn wéi
其安易持，其未兆易谋，其脆易泮，其微易散。为
zhī yú wèi yǒu zhì zhī yú wèi luàn
之于未有，治之于未乱。

hé bào zhī mù shēng yú háo mò jiǔ céng zhī tái qǐ yú lěi tǔ qiān lǐ
合抱之木，生于毫末。九层之台，起于累土。千里
zhī xíng shǐ yú zú xià
之行，始于足下。[①]。

mín zhī cóng shì cháng yú jǐ chéng ér bài zhī shèn zhōng rú shǐ zé wú
民之从事，常于几成而败之。慎终如始，则无
bài shì
败事。

shì yǐ shèng rén yù bù yù bù guì nán dé zhī huò xué bù xué fù zhòng
是以圣人欲不欲，不贵难得之货；学不学，复众
rén zhī suǒ guò yǐ fǔ wàn wù zhī zì rán ér bù gǎn wéi
人之所过，以辅万物之自然，而不敢为。

注释

① 通行本原在“始于足下”后还有“为者败之，执者失之。是以圣人无为，故无败；无执，故无失”一段，但与上下文文义不相关联，疑是与第二十九章错简，故予以删除。

今译

局面安稳的时候容易持守，事情还没有征兆的时候容易谋划。事物脆弱的时候容易分解，事物细微的时候容易消散。要在事情尚未发生之

前早做准备，在祸乱还没有产生之前就进行处理。

合抱的大树，是由细小的萌芽长成的；九层的高台，是由一筐筐泥土堆成的；千里的行程，是从脚下起步的。

人们做事情，往往在快要成功的时候失败。如果在事情快要完成的时候也能像开始时那样慎重，就没有办不成的事。

因此，圣人追求无欲，不看重难得的财物；学别人所不学的，补救众人的过错，以辅助万物自然发展而不妄加干预。

英译

It is easy to maintain the situation when it is stable, and it is easy to plan when there are no signs of things happening yet. When things are fragile, they are easy to break down, and when they are minute, they are easy to dissipate. Act before something happens; govern before chaos arises.

A tree that fills the arms grows from a tiny sprout; a nine-story terrace arises from baskets of earth; a journey of a thousand miles starts beneath the feet.

People usually fail when they are on the verge of success. If one is as cautious at the end as at the beginning, there will be no failure.

Therefore, the sages desire to have no desires, do not value rare goods, learn what others do not learn, remedy the mistakes made by the people, and thus assist the natural development of all things without daring to interfere.

本章主旨

倡导防患于未然，于问题未产生时谋划解决；强调事物发展由小及大，须注重积累、循序渐进；主张顺应自然、无为而治，避免强行干预致败；告诫做事要善始善终，时刻谨慎；建议树立不慕世俗、纠正众人过错的价值观与学习观。

The gist of the chapter

Advocate preventing problems early. Stress that things develop from small to large, so focus on accumulation. Uphold naturalness and non-contrived governance, avoid forceful interference. Warn to be consistent from start to end, stay cautious. Set values shunning fame and correct common mistakes.

本章启示

做事要有前瞻性，防患于未然，将问题解决在萌芽中；重视积累，明白伟大成就源于微小起步，须脚踏实地；顺应自然规律，不过度干预，不执着于结果；做事要善始善终，全程保持谨慎；淡泊名利，不过度追求物质财富；善于自我反思，从他人过错中吸取教训；尊重万物自然本性，辅助其发展，与自然和谐共处。

The enlightenment of the chapter

When engaging in any endeavor, one should be forward-thinking, taking proactive steps to prevent problems and address them at their early stages. Recognize the importance of accumulation, understanding that great achievements have humble beginnings and require a down-to-earth approach. Adhere to the laws of nature, refraining from excessive interference and without being overly attached to outcomes. Ensure that every task is well-initiated and well-completed, maintaining a cautious attitude throughout the process. Cultivate an indifference to fame and fortune, avoiding excessive pursuit of material wealth. Be adept at self-reflection and draw lessons from the mistakes of others. Respect the natural essence of all things, facilitate their development, and strive for harmonious coexistence with nature.

第六十五章

gǔ zhī shàn wéi dào zhě fēi yǐ míng mín jiāng yǐ yú zhī mín zhī nán
古之善为道者，非以明民，将以愚之①。民之难
zhì yǐ qí zhì duō gù yǐ zhì zhì guó guó zhī zéi bù yǐ zhì zhì guó guó
治，以其智多。故以智治国，国之贼；不以智治国，国
zhī fú
之福。

zhī cǐ liǎng zhě yì jī shì héng zhī jī shì shì wèi xuán dé xuán dé shēn
知此两者亦稽式。恒知稽式，是谓玄德。玄德深
yǐ yuǎn yǐ yǔ wù fǎn yǐ nǎi zhì dà shùn
矣，远矣，与物反矣②，乃至大顺。

注释

①“非以明民，将以愚之”中的“愚”并非一般意义上的“愚蠢，愚弄”，在老子思想语境中，“愚”有“返璞归真，去除巧诈智伪”之意。

② 与物反矣：此处理解为“与万物复归真朴”，也有注本解释为“与万物常理相反”。

今译

古代善于遵循“道”来治理的人，不是使民众精明，而是要使民众淳朴。民众之所以难治理，是因为他们的智巧心机太多。所以，用智巧来治理国家，是国家的灾祸；不用智巧来治理国家，是国家的福气。

了解这两种治国方式的差别，也就知道了治国的范式。总是能明白这个范式，就叫作“玄德”。玄奥之德深邃悠远，它与万物复归到真朴，然后才能达到大顺。

英译

Those who were good at following Dao in ancient times did not make the people clever, but made them simple-minded. The reason why the people are difficult to govern is that they are too clever. Therefore, governing a state with cleverness is a disaster for the state; governing the state without cleverness is a blessing for the state.

He who knows the differences between these two modes of governance knows a principle of governance. Constantly keeping this principle is called the mystic De. The mystic De is profound, far-reaching and all things revert back to the natural simplicity. Only then great harmony emerges.

本章主旨

倡导以道治国，让民众保持淳朴，反对以智巧治理，认为智巧是国家灾祸，明白两种治国方式的差异并遵循淳朴之道，即“玄德”，“玄德”能使万物复归真朴，实现顺应自然的理想治理状态。

The gist of the chapter

Advocate governing the state in accordance with Dao, enabling the people to maintain simplicity and honesty. Oppose governing with cleverness and guile, considering them as a disaster for the state. Understanding the differences between the two modes of governance and following the principle of simplicity is called the mystical De. The mystical De can enable all things to return to their natural simplicity, achieving an ideal state of governance that conforms to nature.

本章启示

倡导民众保持质朴，不过分追逐机巧算计，回归内心宁静；治国理政不宜过度依赖智谋，应遵循规律，以维护社会自然和谐；个人与组织须坚守行为准则，践行德行，赢得尊重信任；追求发展要顺应自然，实现经济、社会、环境等多方面和谐统一及可持续发展。

The enlightenment of the chapter

Advocate the public to stay simple, eschew excessive cunning calculations, and regain inner peace. In governance, rely less on wits and strategies; instead, follow the laws to preserve social natural harmony. Both individuals and organizations should abide by codes of conduct, and practice virtues to earn respect and trust. When seeking development, conform to nature for harmonious unity and sustainable development across the economy, society, and the environment.

第六十六章

jiāng hǎi zhī suǒ yǐ néng wéi bǎi gǔ wáng zhě yǐ qí shàn xià zhī gù néng
江海之所以能为百谷王者，以其善下之，故能
wéi bǎi gǔ wáng
为百谷王。

shì yǐ shèng rén yù shàng mín bì yǐ yán xià zhī yù xiān mín bì yǐ
是以圣人欲上民[1]，必以言下之；欲先民，必以
shēn hòu zhī shì yǐ shèng rén chǔ shàng ér mín bù zhòng chǔ qián ér mín bù
身后之。是以圣人处上而民不重，处前而民不
hài shì yǐ tiān xià lè tuī ér bù yàn yǐ qí bù zhēng gù tiān xià mò néng yǔ
害。是以天下乐推而不厌。以其不争，故天下莫能与
zhī zhēng
之争。

注释

① 是以圣人欲上民：王弼本无“圣人”二字，而河上公本、帛书本、竹简本等都有“圣人”二字，故据此校正。

今译

江海之所以能成为百川之王，是因为善于处于低下的位置，所以能成为百川之王。

因此，圣人要想居于民众之上，一定要言辞谦下；要想居于民众之前，一定要身居其后。所以，有道的圣人虽然居于民众之上，民众却不感到有负担；居于民众之前，民众却不感到有妨害。因此，天下的民众都乐意推戴而不会感到厌倦。因为圣人不与民众相争，所以天下没有人能与他相争。

英译

The reason why rivers and seas can become the kings of valley streams is that they are good at staying in a low position. Hence, they are able to be the kings of valley streams.

Therefore, if a sage wants to be above the people, he must be humble in his words towards the people. If a sage wants to be ahead of the people, he must place himself behind the people. Therefore, although the sage is above the people, the people do not feel burdened; although the sage is ahead of the people, the people do not feel harmed. Therefore, all the people under Heaven are willing to support him and will not feel weary. Because he does not contend, no one under Heaven can contend with him.

本章主旨

本章以江海处下成百谷王作比，阐明圣人领导民众应言辞谦下、利益居后，如此方能让民众不觉有负担与妨害而获天下拥戴，强调无私不争，方能无人能与之争。

The gist of the chapter

By comparing rivers and seas, which are in the lower position and become the king of valley streams, this chapter clarifies that the sages, when leading the people, should use humble words and put the people's interests ahead of their own. In this way, the people will not feel burdened or hindered, and the sages will be supported by the whole world. It emphasizes that by being selfless and no contending, no one can compete with them.

本章启示

领导者应谦逊，放低姿态尊重他人，以此赢得拥护；要身先士卒、无私奉献，面对困难勇于担当，获取信任支持；须以民众福祉为出发点，减轻民众负担，造福大众；秉持不争理念，不与下属争功，不与他人争利，营造良好氛围，成就卓越。

The enlightenment of the chapter

Leaders ought to exhibit humility, maintain a modest demeanor, and show respect for others, thereby earning their support. They should lead by example, making selfless contributions, and have the courage to assume responsibilities when confronted with difficulties, thus gaining trust and backing. Taking the people's welfare as the foundation, leaders must strive to lighten their burdens and bring tangible benefits to the public. Moreover, they should adhere to the principle of non-contention, refraining from competing with subordinates for credit or with others for personal interests. By doing so, they can foster a positive environment and attain a high level of excellence.

第六十七章

wǒ yǒu sān bǎo chí ér bǎo zhī yī yuē cí èr yuē jiǎn sān yuē bù gǎn
我有三宝[①]，持而保之。一曰慈，二曰俭，三曰不敢
wéi tiān xià xiān cí gù néng yǒng jiǎn gù néng guǎng bù gǎn wéi tiān xià
为天下先。慈故能勇，俭故能广，不敢为天下
xiān gù néng chéng qì zhǎng jīn shě cí qiě yǒng shě jiǎn qiě guǎng shě hòu
先，故能成器长。今舍慈且勇，舍俭且广，舍后
qiě xiān sǐ yǐ
且先，死矣！

fú cí yǐ zhàn zé shèng yǐ shǒu zé gù tiān jiāng jiù zhī yǐ cí
夫慈，以战则胜，以守则固。天将救之，以慈
wèi zhī
卫之。

注释

① 通行本原有“天下皆谓我：道大，似不肖。夫唯大，故似不肖。若肖，久矣其细也夫”一段，但与下文“我有三宝……”不相关联，疑是与第三十四章错简，故予以删除。

今译

我有三件法宝，持有并保全着。第一是慈爱，第二是节俭，第三是不敢居于天下人前面。因为有了慈爱，所以能勇武；因为有了节俭，所以能富裕；因为不敢居于天下人前面，所以能成为众人的官长。现在人们舍弃慈爱而追求勇武，舍弃节俭而追求富裕，舍弃居后而追求争先，这是走向死路啊！

慈爱，用来征战就能胜利，用来守卫就能巩固。上天要救助谁，就会用慈爱来护卫他。

英译

I have three treasures that I hold and preserve: the first is called benevolence, the second is called frugality, and the third is called not daring to be ahead of others under Heaven. Benevolence enables one to be brave; frugality enables one to be abundant; not daring to be ahead of others under Heaven enables one to be the leader. Now, there are people who abandon benevolence yet pursue only bravery, abandon frugality yet pursue only abundance, abandon staying behind yet pursue only being ahead, and thus they are doomed to failure.

Benevolence, when applied in war, can bring victory; when applied in defense, it can ensure solidity. Those whom Heaven intends to protect will be protected with its benevolence.

本章主旨

本章提出“慈”“俭”“不敢为天下先”三宝，阐述其作用和意义，批判了舍三宝而求“勇”“广”“先”的错误行为，指出“慈”是上天护佑的关键。

The gist of the chapter

This chapter proposes the “three treasures” of benevolence, frugality, and not daring to be ahead of others under Heaven, explains their functions and significance, rebukes the wrongdoings of pursuing bravery, abundance and primacy while abandoning these treasures, and highlights that benevolence is crucial for divine protection.

本章启示

“慈”能激发勇气，让人不畏困难，还可营造和谐人际关系，收获善意与温暖；“俭”倡导合理利用资源，避免物质浪费，同时节省精力，专注个人成长；“不敢为天下先”蕴含领导智慧，能平衡团队利益，赢得信任，也提醒人们保持沉稳，积累实力，待时行动，且秉持低调谦逊，踏实做事，避免麻烦，稳步迈向成功。

The enlightenment of the chapter

“Benevolence” can evoke courage for fearless confrontation with difficulties and cultivate harmonious relationships filled with kindness and warmth. “Frugality” calls for rational resource use to prevent waste, saves energy, and promotes personal growth. “Not daring to be ahead of others under Heaven” reflects leadership wisdom, balancing team interests and earning trust. It also urges people to stay calm, gather strength, act opportunely, be low-key and humble, work steadily, avoid troubles, and progress towards success.

第六十八章

shàn wéi shì zhě bù wǔ shàn zhàn zhě bù nù shàn shèng dí zhě bù
善为士者，不武；善战者，不怒；善胜敌者，不
yǔ shàn yòng rén zhě wèi zhī xià shì wèi bù zhēng zhī dé shì wèi yòng rén
与；善用人者，为之下。是谓不争之德，是谓用人
zhī lì shì wèi pèi tiān gǔ zhī jí
之力，是谓配天古之极。①

注释

① 是谓不争之德，是谓用人之力，是谓配天古之极：帛书本作“是谓不争之德，是谓用人，是谓配天，古之极也”，无“之力”二字。王弼本等作“是谓不争之德，是谓用人之力，是谓配天，古之极”，故据王弼本及俞樾等考证予以修正，使该句式一致、押韵。

今译

善于做将士的人，不崇尚武力；善于打仗的人，不轻易发怒；善于战胜敌人的人，不与敌人交战；善于用人的人，对人谦下。这叫作不与人争的品德，这叫作善于用人，这叫作符合天道——自古就有的最高准则。

英译

A good warrior is not violent; a good fighter is not angry; a good conqueror does not fight; a good user of men abases himself. This is known as the virtue of non-contention, as the ability to utilize the people's talents, as conforming to the Dao of Heaven—the ancient supreme law.

本章主旨

本章通过阐述善为士者不武、善战者不怒、善胜敌者不与、善用人者为之下，倡导不尚武力、以柔克刚的军事与斗争策略，强调谦下用人的管理智慧，将其归结为不与人争、符合自然的德之准则。

The gist of the chapter

By stating that a good warrior isn't violent, a good fighter isn't angry, a good conqueror avoids fighting, and a good employer humbles himself, this chapter promotes military and conflict strategies favoring non-force and using the gentle to overcome the tough. It highlights the wisdom of humility in personnel management, concluding that such practices adhere to the moral principle of non-contention and harmony with nature.

本章启示

处理问题依靠智慧、策略，避免武力强制；学会控制情绪，不被愤怒左右，冷静、理智决策；做事灵活变通，避免正面冲突，以巧妙方式达成目标；秉持谦逊态度，尊重他人，善于纳言，能凝聚力量，赢得支持。

The enlightenment of the chapter

Tackle issues with wisdom and strategy, steadfastly eschewing force and coercion. Masterfully govern your emotions, ensuring not to be swayed by anger, and consistently make composed and rational decisions. Exhibit flexibility in your approach to affairs, deftly sidestepping direct confrontations, and artfully attain your objectives. Embody a spirit of humility, demonstrate profound respect for others, willingly embrace counsel, and adeptly consolidate strength while winning unwavering support.

第六十九章

yòng bīng yǒu yán　wú bù gǎn wéi zhǔ　ér wéi kè　bù gǎn jìn cùn　ér tuì
用兵有言：吾不敢为主，而为客；不敢进寸，而退
chǐ　shì wèi xíng wú háng　rǎng wú bì　zhí wú bīng　rēng wú dí
尺。是谓行无行，攘无臂，执无兵，扔无敌[①]。
huò mò dà yú qīng dí　qīng dí jī sàng wú bǎo　gù kàng bīng xiāng ruò
祸莫大于轻敌，轻敌几丧吾宝。故抗兵相若[②]，
āi zhě shèng yǐ
哀者胜矣。

注释

① 执无兵，扔无敌：王弼本作“扔无敌，执无兵”，此处采用帛书本的句序，句式前后押韵。

② 抗兵相若：通行本作“抗兵相加”。“抗兵相若”意为两军兵力相当。此处按帛书本、傅奕本等校正。

今译

用兵作战有这样的话：“我不敢采取攻势，而采取守势；不敢前进一寸，而宁可后退一尺。”这就是说，虽有阵势，却像没有阵势可摆；虽要振臂，却像没有胳臂可举；虽有兵器，却像没有兵器可持；虽面临敌人，却像没有敌人可打。

祸患没有比轻敌更大的了，轻敌几乎丧失了我的“三宝”。所以，当两军实力相当的时候，怀有慈悲怜悯之心的一方能获得胜利。

英译

There was a saying in the military confrontation："I dare not attack but would rather defend；I dare not advance an inch but would rather retreat a foot." This is called arraying the troops as if no troops could be seen；rolling up sleeves as if no arms could be seen；holding weapons as if no weapons could be seen；confronting the enemy as if no enemy could be seen.

There is no disaster greater than underestimating the enemy. Underestimating the enemy will almost cause me to lose my three treasures. Therefore，when two opposing armies are evenly matched，victory will go to the one that has sorrow on its side.

本章主旨

本章主张军事上以守为攻、以退为进，追求不战而胜的境界，警示轻敌的危害，强调怀有慈悲怜悯之心在战争中的重要性，认为"哀者"在对抗中更易取胜。

The gist of the chapter

The chapter advocates adopting a defensive as offensive and retreat as advance strategy in military affairs，pursuing the realm of winning without fighting，warns of the dangers of underestimating the enemy，emphasizes the importance of having a compassionate and merciful heart in wars，and holds that "the sorrowful" is more likely to win in confrontations.

本章启示

为人处世应谦逊退让，不主动挑起争端，以退为进；时刻保持敬畏，不轻敌，避免骄傲自满致祸；真正的强大源自内心坚定，要透过表象看本质，以柔克刚；心怀慈悲，理解他人，乐于助人，收获信任与内心富足。

The enlightenment of the chapter

In dealing with people and handling affairs, one should be humble and yielding, without taking the initiative to provoke disputes, and use retreat as a means of advance. Always maintain a sense of awe, do not underestimate the enemy, and avoid disasters caused by arrogance and complacency. True strength comes from inner firmness. One should see through the appearance to perceive the essence and use softness to overcome hardness. Be compassionate, understand others, be ready to help others, and gain trust and inner richness.

第七十章

wú yán shèn yì zhī shèn yì xíng tiān xià mò néng zhī mò néng xíng
吾言甚易知，甚易行，天下莫能知，莫能行。
yán yǒu zōng shì yǒu jūn fú wéi wú zhī shì yǐ bù wǒ zhī zhī wǒ zhě xī zé
言有宗，事有君。夫唯无知，是以不我知。知我者希，则
wǒ zhě guì shì yǐ shèng rén pī hè huái yù
我者贵。是以圣人被褐怀玉。

今译

我的话很容易理解，也很容易实行。天下却没有人能理解，没有人能实行。言论有宗旨，行事有根据。正因为无知，所以才不理解我。能理解我的人很少，能效仿我的人就更难得了。因此，圣人总是穿着粗布衣服，怀里揣着美玉。

英译

My words are very easy to understand and put into practice. However, no one in the world can truly understand them or truly put them into practice. Words have a gist, and deeds have a guiding principle. It is just because of people's ignorance that they do not understand me. Those who understand me are rare, and those who follow my example are even rarer. Therefore, the sage wears coarse clothes while carrying jade in his bosom.

本章主旨

老子感慨自己的言论和主张易知难行，强调言行皆有其内在依据，叹息理解和取法自己的人太少，以圣人“被褐怀玉”为例，彰显内在道德智慧比外在表现更重要。

The gist of the chapter

Laozi felt that his words and ideas were easy to understand yet difficult to put into practice. He emphasized that both words and deeds had their internal basis. He sighed that there were too few people who could understand and follow his teachings. Taking the example of a sage who "wears coarse clothes while carrying jade in his bosom", he demonstrated that inner moral wisdom is more important than outward appearance.

本章启示

道理虽易知却难遵行，人们常因外物干扰而无法践行，如生活与经营中应遵循自然规律和内心本真；言论行事须以“道”为宗为君，个人修养与社会治理皆应如此；面对不被理解，要坚持自我价值；同时，莫追求外在虚荣，注重内在修养，如默默奉献于公益事业者，关注精神追求。

The enlightenment of the chapter

Although the principles are inherently straightforward to comprehend, their practical implementation often proves arduous. People are frequently impeded by external influences, preventing them from acting in accordance with these principles. For instance, in daily life and business management, one ought to adhere to the natural laws and the authenticity of one's heart. In both words and deeds, the concept of Dao should serve as the fundamental guiding tenet. This principle is equally applicable to personal self-cultivation and social governance. When confronted with a lack of understanding from others, individuals should steadfastly uphold their own self-worth. Simultaneously, instead of chasing after external vanity, one should direct their focus towards inner spiritual cultivation. Take those who selflessly engage in public welfare endeavors for example. They prioritize spiritual pursuits over material gains and external recognition.

第七十一章

zhī bù zhī shàng yǐ bù zhī zhī bìng yǐ shèng rén bù bìng yǐ qí
知不知[1]，上矣。不知知，病矣。圣人不病，以其
bìng bìng shì yǐ bù bìng
病病，是以不病。[2]

注释

① 知不知：此处解释为“知道却不自以为知道”，这是圣人谦逊的写照。另一种解释为“知道自己不知道”。

② 圣人不病，以其病病，是以不病：王弼本作“夫唯病病，是以不病。圣人不病，以其病病，是以不病”，文句似颠倒且重复，故据帛书本等校正。“夫唯”之句，常承上句之意而重言之，此为老子《道德经》特有文例，如“夫唯弗居，是以不去”“夫唯不争，故无尤”“夫唯不盈，故能蔽而新成”“夫唯不厌，是以不厌”等。

今译

知道却不自以为知道，这是高明；不知道却自以为知道，这是弊病。圣人没有这种弊病，因为他把这种弊病当作弊病，所以才不会有弊病。

英译

To know yet not claim to know is wise. Not to know yet claim to know is a flaw. The sage doesn't have the flaw because he regards such a flaw as a flaw. Hence he is free from it.

本章主旨

本章倡导“知不知”的谦逊认知态度，批判“不知知”的弊病，强调正视自身不足、以自省来实现自我完善，借圣人无弊病的例子为人们树立修身标杆。

The gist of the chapter

This chapter advocates the humble cognitive stance of “knowing yet not claiming to know”, while criticizing the perils of “not knowing yet pretending to know”. It highlights the significance of squarely facing one’s own deficiencies and attaining self-improvement via self-reflection. And it sets a standard for self-cultivation by presenting the example of sages who are devoid of such flaws.

本章启示

要保持谦逊求知，意识到自身知识局限，不断探索；切不可不懂装懂，以免阻碍成长与决策；要正视自身问题，视其为弊病并积极改正；效仿圣人，将自我反思与完善当作习惯，助力个人良好发展。

The enlightenment of the chapter

One ought to uphold a humble demeanor and an insatiable thirst for learning, being fully cognizant of the boundaries of one’s knowledge and perpetually engaged in exploration. Under no circumstances should one feign knowledge in areas where one is ignorant, for such pretense can stymie both personal growth and sound decision-making. Have the courage to confront one’s own issues, perceiving them as areas for improvement, and take proactive steps to rectify them. Draw inspiration from the sages by making self-reflection and continuous self-enhancement an ingrained habit and a practice that will significantly propel one’s personal development.

第七十二章

mín bù wèi wēi　zé dà wēi zhì　wú xiá qí suǒ jū　wú yàn qí suǒ shēng
民不畏威，则大威至。无狎其所居，无厌其所生。
fú wéi bù yàn　shì yǐ bù yàn　shì yǐ shèng rén zì zhī bù zì xiàn　zì ài bù zì
夫唯不厌，是以不厌。是以圣人自知不自见，自爱不自
guì
贵。①

注释

① 通行本本章末还有“故去彼取此”一句，同第十二章注释，疑是后人添加，与前文“是以”句子的意思有重复之嫌，语义、修辞累赘，不符合老子简练风格。

今译

人民不畏惧统治者的威压，那么大的祸乱就要到来了。不要侵扰人民的居所，不要压榨人民的生计。只有不压榨人民，人民才不会厌恶统治者。因此，圣人有自知之明，但不自我表现；有自爱之心，但不自显高贵。

英译

When the people no longer fear the authorities of the rulers, then great disasters are about to befall. Do not encroach upon the people's dwellings, and do not oppress the people's means of livelihood. Only when the people are not oppressed will they not loathe the rulers. Therefore, the sage has self-awareness but does not seek to show off, has self-love but does not seek to exalt himself.

本章主旨

本章从政治角度告诫统治者勿压迫百姓，要为其创造安居环境以获民心；从个人角度倡导人们要有自知自爱、不自我显耀的修身理念。

The gist of the chapter

From a political perspective, this chapter admonishes rulers against oppressing the common folk. Instead, they are urged to foster a peaceful living milieu for the people, thereby winning their hearts and support. From an individual standpoint, it espouses the self-cultivation tenets of self-awareness, self-love, and the conscious avoidance of flaunting oneself.

本章启示

权力运用上，威压过度易致反抗，应避免。人际关系中，须给予他人生存空间与自由，不可过度挤压；互动遵循相互性原则，尊重他人才能获他人尊重。个人修养方面，要关注自我认知与内在提升，不图虚荣，如此方能赢得认可与尊重。

The enlightenment of the chapter

When exercising power, excessive coercion is apt to trigger resistance and must be eschewed. In interpersonal relations, it is essential to afford others ample living space and freedom, refraining from over-encroachment. During interactions, abide by the principle of reciprocity. Only through respecting others can one hope to receive respect in return. Regarding personal cultivation, one should center on self-awareness and inner enhancement, shunning vanity, so as to gain due recognition and respect.

第七十三章

yǒng yú gǎn zé shā　yǒng yú bù gǎn zé huó　cǐ liǎng zhě huò lì huò hài
勇于敢则杀，勇于不敢则活。[①]此两者或利或害。
tiān zhī suǒ wù　shú zhī qí gù
天之所恶，孰知其故？[②]

tiān zhī dào　bù zhēng ér shàn shèng　bù yán ér shàn yìng　bù zhào ér zì
天之道，不争而善胜，不言而善应，不召而自
lái　chǎn rán ér shàn móu　tiān wǎng huī huī　shū ér bù shī
来，繟然而善谋。天网恢恢，疏而不失。

注释

① 勇于敢则杀，勇于不敢则活：此处“敢”与“不敢”分别解释为“坚强”与“柔弱”，与第七十六章“坚强者死之徒，柔弱者生之徒”对应。

② 通行本第一段段末还有“是以圣人犹难之”一句，而帛书本等则无此句。据高亨等考证，疑是与第六十三章错简重出，故予以删除。

今译

勇于坚强就会死，勇于柔弱就可活。这两者有的有利，有的有害。上天所厌恶的，谁能知晓其中缘由？

天道就是，不争斗而善于获胜，不言语而善于回应，不召唤而自动到来，坦然自若而善于谋划。天网广大无边，看似疏松却不会有任何漏失。

英译

Bravery in daring to be hard and strong leads to death; bravery in daring to be soft and weak survives. Of these two, one is beneficial and the other is harmful. What Heaven loathes, who can know the reason behind it?

The Dao of Heaven is good at winning without contending and responding without speaking, comes on its own without being called, and it is good at planning with calm. The net of Heaven is broad and loose, but nothing escapes.

本章主旨

辩证看待“勇”，指出不同“勇”的结果差异；表达对天道的敬畏，强调其不可全知；阐释天道特性，如不争而胜、不言而应等；借“天网恢恢”劝人顺应天道，依循规律行事。

The gist of the chapter

View “bravery” dialectically, pointing out the differences in the outcomes of different kinds of “bravery”; express awe for the Dao of Heaven, emphasizing that it cannot be fully understood; expound on the characteristics of the Dao of Heaven, such as winning without contending, responding without words, etc.; by citing “the net of Heaven is broad and loose, but nothing escapes”, persuade people to conform to the Dao of Heaven and act in accordance with the laws.

本章启示

其一，勇有两面，盲目蛮干不可取，审慎克制才是真勇，影响行为成败；其二，自然规律复杂难测，人应敬畏它，勿主观臆断；其三，倡导无为智慧，不争不躁，顺应规律做事，反而易收获成果；其四，强调因果与公正，世间有法则，行为皆有报，人当坚守道德，对己负责。

The enlightenment of the chapter

Firstly, bravery has two sides. Blind and reckless action is not advisable; prudence and self-restraint are the true essence of bravery, which influence the success or failure of actions. Secondly, the laws of nature are complex and unpredictable. People should hold them in awe and avoid making subjective assumptions. Thirdly, advocate the wisdom of "wu-wei" (non-action). By refraining from contention and impatience and acting in accordance with the laws, it is easier to achieve results. Fourthly, emphasize cause-and-effect and justice. There are rules in the world, and every action has its consequences. People should uphold morality and be responsible for themselves.

第七十四章

mín bù wèi sǐ nài hé yǐ sǐ jù zhī ruò shǐ mín héng wèi sǐ ér wéi jī
民不畏死，奈何以死惧之。若使民恒畏死，而为奇
zhě wú dé zhí ér shā zhī shú gǎn
者，吾得执而杀之，孰敢。

héng yǒu sī shā zhě shā fú dài sī shā zhě shā shì dài dà jiàng zhuó fú
恒有司杀者杀。夫代司杀者杀，是代大匠斫。夫
dài dà jiàng zhuó zhě xī yǒu bù shāng qí shǒu yǐ
代大匠斫者，希有不伤其手矣。

今译

人民不畏惧死亡，为什么要用死亡来吓唬他们呢？如果使人民总是畏惧死亡，那么对于那些为邪作恶的人，就可以抓来杀掉，那还有谁敢为非作歹呢？

总是有行刑官（天道）来主管杀人。那些代替行刑官去杀人的，就如同代替木匠去砍木头一样。那些代替木匠砍木头的人，很少有不砍伤自己手的。

英译

If the people do not fear death, why threaten them with it? If the people are always made to fear death, I could catch those who do wrong and put them into death. Who would then dare to do wrong?

There is always the executioner (the Dao of Heaven) who is in charge of the killing. He who does the killing in place of the executioner is like hewing wood in place of the master carpenter, and seldom escape hurting his own hands.

本章主旨

批判统治者以死惧民的严刑峻法，强调应顺应自然，上天自有司杀之理，警示统治者勿越俎代庖、滥用权力，否则易自伤。

The gist of the chapter

Criticize the rulers' harsh laws and severe punishments that instill fear of death among the people. Emphasize the need to conform to nature, for there is a natural order of judgment by the Dao of Heaven. Warn the rulers not to overstep their bounds and abuse their power; otherwise, they are likely to bring harm to themselves.

本章启示

治理中，单用死刑威慑走投无路的民众难达目的，易激民愤；管理者应遵循客观规律，不过度干预，如同尊重市场规律；要关注民生，让民众安居乐业，以使社会稳定；同时，依法惩处违法者，维护公正秩序，但不可滥用权力。

The enlightenment of the chapter

In governance, solely using the death penalty to intimidate desperate people is unlikely to achieve the desired goals and may easily arouse public anger. Managers should follow objective laws and refrain from excessive intervention, just as they respect market laws. They should pay attention to people's livelihoods, enabling the public to live and work in peace and contentment, so that society can remain stable. At the same time, law-breakers should be punished in accordance with the law to maintain a just order, but the abuse of power should be avoided.

第七十五章

mín zhī jī yǐ qí shàng shí shuì zhī duō shì yǐ jī mín zhī nán zhì yǐ
民之饥，以其上食税之多，是以饥。民之难治，以
qí shàng zhī yǒu wéi shì yǐ nán zhì mín zhī qīng sǐ yǐ qí shàng shēng shēng
其上之有为，是以难治。民之轻死，以其上生生
zhī hòu shì yǐ qīng sǐ fú wéi wú yǐ shēng wéi zhě shì xián yú guì shēng
之厚，是以轻死。夫唯无以生为者，是贤于贵生。

今译

人民之所以饥饿，是因为统治者的赋税太多，所以人民才会饥饿。人民之所以难以治理，是因为统治者强作妄为，所以才难以管理。人民之所以轻视死亡，是因为统治者奉养奢华，所以人民才看轻死亡。只有那些不追求优厚生活的人，才比奉养奢华的人高明。

英译

The people are starved because of too much taxes imposed by the rulers. That is why they are starved. The people are difficult to rule because their rulers are too meddlesome. That is why they are difficult to rule. The people take death lightly because their rulers live in too great luxury. That is why they take death lightly. Only those who do not care for their lives are wiser than those who take much care of their lives.

本章主旨

本章揭示百姓困苦及社会乱象源于统治者苛政与贪奢，倡导统治者

无为而治，批判过度追求物质享受的价值观，推崇顺应自然、不过度求生的高尚理念。

The gist of the chapter

The chapter reveals that the hardships of the common people and the chaos in society stem from the rulers' harsh policies, avarice, and extravagance. It advocates that rulers should practice governance by non-interference, criticizes the values of excessive pursuit of material enjoyment, and extols the noble concept of conforming to nature and not overly striving for survival.

本章启示

社会治理上，要关注民生，合理征税，避免民众因税负重而饥饿；减少行政干预，无为而治，让社会自然发展；注重公平，防止统治者因厚己薄民而导致社会矛盾频发。个人修养上，应看淡物质享受，追求精神富足；树立正确生死观，顺应自然，珍惜当下。

The enlightenment of the chapter

In social governance, it is necessary to pay attention to people's livelihood, levy taxes reasonably, and avoid making people suffer from hunger due to heavy tax burdens. Reduce administrative intervention, govern by non-action, and let society develop naturally. Emphasize fairness and prevent rulers from favoring themselves over the people, which could lead to social conflicts.

In terms of personal cultivation, one should not over-value material enjoyment but pursue spiritual richness. One should establish a correct view of life and death, conform to nature, and cherish the present moment.

第七十六章

rén zhī shēng yě róu ruò qí sǐ yě jiān qiáng cǎo mù zhī shēng yě róu cuì
人之生也柔弱，其死也坚强。草木之生也柔脆，
qí sǐ yě kū gǎo gù jiān qiáng zhě sǐ zhī tú róu ruò zhě shēng zhī tú shì yǐ
其死也枯槁。故坚强者死之徒，柔弱者生之徒。是以
bīng qiáng zé miè mù qiáng zé shé jiān qiáng chǔ xià róu ruò chǔ shàng
兵强则灭，木强则折。坚强处下①，柔弱处上。

注释

① 坚强处下：通行本作“强大处下”，傅奕本、景龙碑本等作“坚强处下”，此处作“坚强处下”与前文对应，符合文义和逻辑。

今译

人活着的时候身体是柔软的，死后就变得僵硬了。草木生长的时候是柔脆的，死后就变得干枯了。所以，坚强的东西属于死亡的一类，柔弱的东西属于生存的一类。因此，用兵逞强就会遭受灭亡，树木坚硬就会折断。强硬的处在下位，柔弱的反而处在上位。

英译

When alive, human bodies are soft; after death they become hard and stiff. When alive, grass and trees are soft and supple, when dead they become dry and withered. Therefore, the hard and strong belong to the realm of death, while the soft and weak belong to the realm of life.

Hence when an army becomes strong, it will be defeated; when a tree grows strong, it will be broken. The hard and strong are in a disadvantaged position, while the soft and weak are in an advantaged position.

本章主旨

本章通过人、草木等生死时柔刚状态的对比，阐明“柔弱胜刚强”的道理，借此对治国与为人处世予以警示，反对强硬武力，倡导以柔克刚，强调顺应自然规律才能长久。

The gist of the chapter

By comparing the states of softness and hardness in the life and death of humans, plants, etc., this chapter expounds the principle that "the soft and weak overcome the strong and hard". Using this as a means, it warns about the governance and ways of conducting oneself in society, opposes the use of brute force, advocates overcoming the tough with the gentle, and emphasizes that only by conforming to the laws of nature can things endure.

本章启示

强调以柔克刚智慧，如水滴石穿，温和处事更容易解决问题；倡导谦逊低调，强大时不骄傲，如此才能赢得支持；提醒避免僵化，保持灵活；引导重新审视力量，刚柔并济方为长久之道。

The enlightenment of the chapter

The chapter emphasizes the wisdom of using softness to overcome hardness. Just like water dripping wears away the stone, dealing with things in a gentle way makes it easier to solve problems. It advocates being humble and keeping a low profile. One can win support only by not being arrogant when powerful. It reminds people to avoid rigidity and remain flexible. It also guides people to re-examine the concept of strength, and points out that the integration of toughness and gentleness is the way to last.

第七十七章

tiān zhī dào qí yóu zhāng gōng yú gāo zhě yì zhī xià zhě jǔ zhī yǒu
天之道，其犹张弓欤？高者抑之，下者举之；有
yú zhě sǔn zhī bù zú zhě bǔ zhī tiān zhī dào sǔn yǒu yú ér bǔ bù zú rén
余者损之，不足者补之。天之道，损有余而补不足。人
zhī dào zé bù rán sǔn bù zú yǐ fèng yǒu yú
之道则不然，损不足以奉有余。

shú néng yǒu yú yǐ fèng tiān xià wéi yǒu dào zhě shì yǐ shèng rén wéi ér
孰能有余以奉天下？唯有道者。是以圣人为而
bù shì gōng chéng ér bù chǔ qí bù yù xiàn xián
不恃，功成而不处。其不欲见贤。

今译

天道不正像拉弓弦吗？弦位高了就把它压低些，弦位低了就把它抬高些；多余了就加以减少，不足了就加以补充。天道就是减少多余的，用来补充不足的。而人类的法则却不是这样，是减少不足的，用来供奉有余的人。

谁能够把有余的拿来供给天下呢？只有有道的人才能做到。因此，圣人施与成全而不自恃己能，有所成就而不自居有功。他不想表现出自己的贤能。

英译

Isn't the Dao of Heaven like drawing a bow? The high it presses down; the low it lifts up. The excessive it reduces; the insufficient it supplements. The Dao of Heaven reduces the excessive and supplements the insufficient. The way of man is different. It reduces the insufficient and supplements the excessive.

Who can take what is excessive and use it to serve the world? Only one who follows Dao can do so. Therefore, the sage promotes things without boasting of his own ability, and accomplishes things without claiming his credits. He has no desire to show his virtue.

本章主旨

本章通过对比“天之道，损有余而补不足”与“人之道，损不足以奉有余”，批判社会不公，倡导有道者遵循天道，不居功自傲，以推动社会公平和谐。

The gist of the chapter

By contrasting “the Dao of Heaven reduces the excessive and supplements the insufficient” with “the way of man reduces the insufficient and supplements the excessive”, the chapter criticizes social injustice, and advocates that those who follow Dao should conform to the Dao of Heaven, and they should not be arrogant about their achievements, so as to promote social fairness and harmony.

本章启示

在社会治理上，倡导追求公平，合理调节资源分配，管理者应无私为民谋福祉；在个人修养上，强调保持谦逊，不居功自傲，树立正确价值观，不过分逐利，注重精神富足与分享奉献。

The enlightenment of the chapter

In social governance, the pursuit of fairness and rational adjustment of resource distribution are advocated. Governors should selflessly strive for the people's well-being. As for personal cultivation, it is emphasized to maintain humility, refrain from taking credit and being arrogant, establish a correct value system, avoid over-pursuing material gains, and instead focus on spiritual enrichment, sharing, and dedication.

第七十八章

tiān xià mò róu ruò yú shuǐ ér gōng jiān qiáng zhě mò zhī néng shèng yǐ
天下莫柔弱于水，而攻坚强者莫之能胜，以
qí wú yǐ yì zhī ruò zhī shèng qiáng róu zhī shèng gāng tiān xià mò bù zhī
其无以易之①。弱之胜强，柔之胜刚，天下莫不知，
mò néng xíng
莫能行。

shì yǐ shèng rén yún shòu guó zhī gòu shì wèi shè jì zhǔ shòu guó bù
是以圣人云："受国之垢，是谓社稷主。受国不
xiáng shì wèi tiān xià wáng zhèng yán ruò fǎn
祥，是谓天下王。"正言若反。

注释

① 以其无以易之：通行本作"其无以易之"。蒋锡昌等认为"以其"二字为老子习用之语。此处按帛书本校正。

今译

天下没有比水更柔弱的了，而攻克坚强的东西没有能胜过水的，因为没有什么能替代它。弱能胜强，柔能胜刚，天下没有人不知道这个道理，但没有人能付诸实行。

所以，有道的圣人说："承受国家的屈辱，才称得上国家的君主。承受国家的祸灾，才配做天下的君王。"正面的话好像反说一样。

英译

Nothing in the world is softer than water. However, nothing can surpass it in attacking the hard and strong, for nothing can replace it. Everyone knows that the weak can overcome the strong and the soft can overcome the hard, but no one can put it into practice.

Therefore, the sage once said: "One who can bear the humiliations of the state is worthy of being the sovereign of the state; one who can take on the misfortunes of the state is worthy of being the king of the world." Truthful words seem paradoxical.

本章主旨

本章借水阐释以柔克刚之理，批判知而不行现象，点明统治者应具承受国家屈辱与灾难的担当，同时以“正言若反”揭示语言与真理的辩证关系。

The gist of the chapter

By taking water as an example, this chapter expounds the principle that the weak can overcome the strong, and criticizes the common phenomenon where people are aware of this truth but fail to act upon it. It highlights that rulers ought to possess the courage to shoulder the humiliation and disasters befalling the country. Meanwhile, the saying "truthful words seem paradoxical" unveils the dialectical relationship between language and truth, suggesting that profound truths often appear contrary to common perception.

本章启示

以柔克刚，如以水为鉴，柔和迂回常能解决难题；知行合一，虽知柔能胜刚之理，更需践行；担当领导，领导者应勇于担责，如此方能服众；辩证思维，要突破常规认知，深入理解与常理相悖却蕴含真理的观点。

The enlightenment of the chapter

Overcome the hard with the soft. Just as water demonstrates, employing a gentle and roundabout strategy can frequently resolve intricate problems. Truly integrate knowledge with action. Despite our awareness of the principle that the soft prevails over the hard, it is essential to translate this understanding into practical deeds. Shoulder leadership responsibilities. A leader must have the courage to take on arduous tasks and challenges, thereby earning the trust and support of the people. Adopt a dialectical mindset. We should transcend conventional thinking patterns and delve deep into perspectives that may seem paradoxical at first glance but actually embody profound truths.

第七十九章

hé dà yuàn　bì yǒu yú yuàn　ān kě yǐ wéi shàn　shì yǐ shèng rén zhí zuǒ
和大怨，必有余怨。安可以为善？是以圣人执左

qì　ér bù zé yú rén　yǒu dé sī qì　wú dé sī chè
契[①]而不责于人。有德司契，无德司彻[②]。

tiān dào wú qīn　héng yǔ shàn rén
天道无亲，恒与善人。

注释

① 左契：此处解释为“借据的存根”。

② 司彻：“彻”是周代的税法。

今译

和解深重的怨恨，一定还会有余怨。这怎么能算是妥善的办法呢？因此，圣人保存着借据的存根，但并不向人索取偿还。有德之人就像持有借据的人那样宽容，无德之人就像掌管税收的人那样催逼苛取。

天道没有偏爱，总是与善人一起。

英译

When a great animosity is reconciled, there is bound to be some remaining resentment. How can this be regarded as a good way? Therefore, the sage keeps an evidence of debt but does not demand repayment with harsh words. A person of virtue is as tolerant as one who holds an evidence of debt, while a person without virtue presses for and exacts harshly, just like a tax collector.

The Dao of Heaven shows no favoritism, but it is always on the side of the good people.

本章主旨

反思“和大怨”存在的不足，倡导以宽容代替苛责，通过对比有德之人与无德之人的行为，强调德的重要性，同时指出天道公正，会佑助善人。

The gist of the chapter

Upon reflecting on the inherent shortcomings of “reconciling a great enmity”, it becomes evident that such efforts often leave behind residual resentment. Thus, it is advocated that we substitute harsh criticism with a spirit of tolerance. By comparing the actions of the virtuous, who, like holders of an evidence of debt, exhibit leniency and refrain from pressing for repayment, with those of the non-virtuous, who, akin to exacting tax collectors, engage in relentless and harsh demands, we can clearly emphasize the significance of virtue. Simultaneously, it must be pointed out that the Dao of Heaven is inherently just and will invariably bestow its blessings upon the kind-hearted.

本章启示

社会治理上，要注重防微杜渐，从源头减少矛盾，执政者须宽容施政。人际交往中，倡导以宽容化解恩怨，不过分苛求他人。个人修养方面，鼓励善良的态度，顺应自然规律，坚守道德底线，豁达面对得失。

The enlightenment of the chapter

In social governance, it's crucial to detect and address problems at their incipient stages, minimizing the root causes of conflicts. Rulers ought to exercise governance with tolerance. In interpersonal interactions, resolving grudges through tolerance is recommended, and one should refrain from being overly exacting towards others. For personal cultivation, individuals are urged to uphold kindness, follow the laws of nature, maintain moral integrity, and embrace an open-minded approach when facing gains and losses.

第八十章

xiǎo guó guǎ mín shǐ yǒu shí bǎi zhī qì ér bù yòng shǐ mín zhòng sǐ ér
小国寡民，使有什佰之器[①]而不用，使民重死而
yuǎn xǐ suī yǒu zhōu yú wú suǒ chéng zhī suī yǒu jiǎ bīng wú suǒ chén
远徙[②]。虽有舟舆，无所乘之；虽有甲兵，无所陈
zhī shǐ mín fù jié shéng ér yòng zhī gān qí shí měi qí fú ān qí jū lè
之。使民复结绳而用之，甘其食，美其服，安其居，乐
qí sú lín guó xiāng wàng jī quǎn zhī shēng xiāng wén mín zhì lǎo sǐ bù
其俗。邻国相望，鸡犬之声相闻，民至老死不
xiāng wǎng lái
相往来。

注释

① 什佰之器：此处解释为“复杂的器具”。河上公本和帛书甲、乙本作“什佰人之器”，高明等理解为“十倍、百倍人工之器”。

② 远徙：许抗生认为，帛书本作“远徙”，通行本等诸本都作“不远徙”，“不”字疑为后人增加，“重”与“远”为对文，皆为动词，故据此校正。

今译

国家规模小，人口稀少。即使有复杂的器具也不使用，使人们看重生死，远离迁徙。虽有船只车辆，却没必要乘坐；虽有铠甲兵器，却没必要陈列。使人们回归结绳记事，吃得香甜，穿得漂亮，住得安适，习俗呈欢。国与国之间互相望得见，鸡鸣犬吠声相互听得到，但人们直到老死也不互相往来。

英译

A small state has a small population. The people there may have various tools, but they do not use them. The people take death seriously and do not travel far. There are boats and carriages, but people have no occasion to ride in them. There are armors and weapons, but there is no need to display them. Let people return to the use of knotted ropes for keeping records. Let them find their food sweet, their clothes beautiful, their dwellings comfortable, and their customs enjoyable. Neighboring states are within sight to each other, and the sounds of cocks crowing and dogs barking can be heard each other; yet the people there, until they grow old and die, do not deal with each other.

本章主旨

本章描绘了“小国寡民”的理想社会形态，反思物质文明，强调精神满足，主张有限的社会交往，倡导回归自然、质朴、宁静的生活。

The gist of the chapter

This chapter vividly depicts the ideal social form of “a small state with a small population”. Through this portrayal, it conducts a profound reflection on material civilization, highlighting the significance of spiritual fulfillment. It actively advocates for a curtailment of excessive social interactions, instead promoting a reversion to a life that is in harmony with nature, simple in lifestyle, and imbued with peace.

本章启示

倡导回归简单本真，摆脱物质繁杂，关注内心需求；珍视本地传统，扎根本土，传承文化；强调适度发展，平衡科技进步与日常生活；反思人际交往，把握社交节奏与边界，保留个人空间并适度与外界联系。

The enlightenment of the chapter

Advocate a return to simplicity and genuineness, casting off the complexities of material pursuits and focusing intently on inner requirements. Deeply cherish local traditions, firmly take root in the local community, and assiduously inherit cultural legacies. Stress the importance of moderate development to strike a balance and maintain harmony between technological progress and daily life. Engage in profound reflection on interpersonal relationships, precisely grasp the rhythm and boundaries of social interactions, safeguard personal space, and sustain appropriate connections with the external world.

第八十一章

xìn yán bù měi　měi yán bù xìn　shàn zhě bù biàn　biàn zhě bù shàn　zhì
信言不美，美言不信。善者不辩，辩者不善。知
zhě bù bó　bó zhě bù zhì
者不博，博者不知。①

shèng rén bù jī　jì yǐ wèi rén　jǐ yù yǒu　jì yǐ yǔ rén　jǐ yù duō
圣人不积，既以为人，己愈有；既以与人，己愈多。
tiān zhī dào　lì ér bù hài　shèng rén zhī dào　wèi ér bù zhēng
天之道，利而不害。圣人之道②，为而不争。

注释

① 知者不博，博者不知：此处解释为“智慧的人不广博，广博的人不智慧”，也有注本将其解释为“智慧的人不争斗，争斗的人不智慧”。

② 圣人之道：帛书本作“人之道”。老子主要是以“圣人”的品行修为作为效法榜样，故据此校正。

今译

诚信的话不华美，华美的话不诚信。善良的人不巧辩，巧辩的人不善良。智慧的人不广博，广博的人不智慧。圣人不私自积藏，尽量帮助别人，自己反而更富有；尽量给予别人，自己反而更充足。天道是利万物而不妨害；圣人之道是施惠于人而不相争。

英译

Truthful words are not fine-sounding. Fine-sounding words are not truthful. Good people do not argue; argumentative people are not good. The wise are not extensively learned; the extensively learned are not wise.

The sages do not accumulate for themselves. The more they do for others, the more they have. The more they give to others, the more they possess. The Dao of Heaven is to benefit without harming. The way of the sage is to act without contending.

本章主旨

本章强调了认知与表达的辩证关系，告诫勿被华丽言辞迷惑，注重实质，真正的善与知并非靠争辩和博杂体现；阐述圣人无私奉献，助人即助己，给予反更富足；总结天道利而不害，圣人之道为而不争，倡导积极作为，同时保持平和，不与人争名夺利。

The gist of the chapter

This chapter emphasizes the dialectical relationship between cognition and expression, warning people not to be misled by flowery words but to focus on substance. True kindness and wisdom are not demonstrated through argumentation and superficial general knowledge. It expounds on the selfless dedication of sages, stating that helping others is equivalent to helping oneself, and dedication actually leads to greater self-abundance. It summarizes that the Dao of Heaven is to benefit without harming, and the way of sages is to act without contending. It advocates taking positive actions while maintaining a peaceful state of mind, and refraining from competing with others for fame and fortune.

本章启示

言语上，勿被华丽言辞迷惑，注重真实可靠。品德修养要重行动，以实际行动践行善良，而非靠言辞标榜。学习工作应追求专精，在特定领域深入钻研。人际交往懂得分享给予，助人同时成就自身。处世秉持利他态度，不与人争名夺利，保持平和心态，专注成长与贡献。

The enlightenment of the chapter

In matters of discourse, eschew rhetorical delusions and anchor communication in verifiable truth and ethical reliability. For moral cultivation, prioritize ethical conduct over verbal assertions, manifesting benevolence through concrete actions rather than ostentatious proclamations. In scholarship and labor, pursue mastery through profound specialization rather than superficial breadth. In social engagement, cultivate generosity as a means of reciprocal self-realization: enriching others inherently enhances one's own spiritual abundance. In worldly dealings, adhere to the principle of selfless beneficence, eschewing rivalry for material gains. Maintain a tranquil equanimity focused on inward cultivation and contributing to collective well-being.

附录

一、道的本体性

（一）道作为宇宙本原的双重维度

《道德经》通过“无—有”辩证框架确立道的本体论定位。第一章以“无”（天地之始）与“有”（万物之母）构成道的双重显现维度，二者“同出而异名”（第一章），在“玄之又玄”（第一章）的终极统合中成为“众妙之门”（第一章）。第四、六、二十五、五十二、六十二章通过“万物之宗”“天地根”“天下母”等喻象，确证道“独立而不改”（第二十五章）的绝对本体性——既是空间维度的万物本宗（“渊兮”，第四章），亦是时间维度的永恒存在（“谷神不死”，第六章）。

道的生成论体系由第四十、四十二、五十一章完成建构：“天下万物生于有，有生于无”（第四十章）确立“无→有→万物”的三阶生成序列；“道生一”（第四十二章）揭示道体通过阴阳冲气（“冲气以为和”，第四十二章）的辩证运动实现万物化生；“道生之，德畜之”（第五十一章）则构建了“道—德—物—器”的生成链条。道的创生具有非意志性特征：虽“万物恃之以生”（第三十四章），却“生而不有，为而不恃”（第五十一章），通过“衣养万物而不为主”（第三十四章）的隐默方式维系宇宙秩序，形成“道法自然”（第二十五章）的非主宰性创生范式。

Ⅰ. The Ontological Nature of Dao

(1) The Dual Dimensions of Dao as the Cosmic Origin

Dao De Jing establishes the ontological positioning of Dao through the dialectical framework of non-being and being. Chapter 1 constructs

Dao's dual manifest dimensions with "non-being" (the origin of Heaven and Earth) and "being" (the Mother of all things), which "are both from the same source but given different names" (Chapter 1). In their ultimate unity of "the mystery of mysteries" (Chapter 1), they constitute the "gateway to all wonders" (Chapter 1). Chapters 4, 6, 25, 52, and 62 employ metaphors such as "the origin of all things", "the root of Heaven and Earth", and "the Mother of the world" to affirm the Dao's absolute ontological nature as "independent and unchanging" (Chapter 25)—it is both the spatial origin of all things ("boundlessness", Chapter 4) and the temporal perpetuity ("the Valley Spirit never dies", Chapter 6).

Dao's cosmogonic system is articulated in Chapters 40, 42, and 51: "All things under Heaven are born from being, and being is born from non-being" (Chapter 40) establishes the three-stage generative sequence of "non-being → being → all things"; "Dao gives birth to One" (Chapter 42) reveals Dao's generation of all things through the dialectical interaction of yin-yang qi ("the two forces of yin and yang interact and blend, thus attaining a state of harmony", Chapter 42); "Dao creates all things, and De nurtures them" (Chapter 51) constructs the generative chain of "Dao – De – Things – Forms". Unlike the volitional creators in religious traditions, Dao's generation is non-volitional: though "all things depend on it for life" (Chapter 34), it "creates all things without possessing them, and promotes all things without relying its ability" (Chapter 51), sustaining cosmic order through the silent mode of "nurturing all things without being their master" (Chapter 34). This forms a non-dominant generative paradigm of "the law of Dao is natural" (Chapter 25).

（二）道的超验性认知困境

《道德经》通过直观体认描述方式揭示道的本体论特征。第四章"道冲"彰显其非实体性（"用之或不盈"），第十四章"夷—希—微"三象论证其超感官性（"不可致诘"），第二十一章"惚恍—窈冥"勾勒其超验实在的认知样态。这种认知困境源于道的双重本体属性——既是

“有物混成”（第二十五章）的绝对实在，又具“无状之状”（第十四章）的不可对象化特质。文本建构的“形上—形下”认知鸿沟体现为：道的“寂寥”（第二十五章）特性否定时空定位（“迎之不见其首”，第十四章），其“泛兮左右”（第三十四章）的遍在性又突破有限性认知框架。这种悖反性表明：道作为“终极奥秘”（第十四章），只能通过否定性范畴（无形/无状/无声）进行指涉，在“不知其名”（第二十五章）的认识论困境中确证其形而上的本体地位。

(2) The Transcendental Cognitive Dilemma of Dao

Dao De Jing reveals Dao's ontological characteristics through intuitive apprehension: "Dao is void" (Chapter 4) highlights its non-substantiality ("its use is inexhaustible"), the threefold imagery of "invisible – inaudible – intangible" in Chapter 14 attests to its nature of imperceptibility ("unfathomable"), and "profound and obscure" in Chapter 21 outlines the cognitive modality of its transcendental reality. This dilemma stems from Dao's dual ontological attributes: it is both the absolute reality of "something as an integrated whole" (Chapter 25) and the non-objectifiable quality of "the form of formless" (Chapter 14). The text constructs a "metaphysical – physical" cognitive chasm: Dao's "soundless and formless" (Chapter 25) nature negates spatiotemporal localization ("greeting it, one cannot see its front", Chapter 14), while its omnipresence of "pervading all around" (Chapter 34) surpasses finite cognitive frameworks. This paradox signifies that Dao, as the "ultimate mystery" (Chapter 14), can only be referenced through negative categories (formless/shapeless/soundless), confirming its metaphysical ontological status amid the epistemological predicament of "not knowing its name" (Chapter 25).

（三）道的语言超越性特质

《道德经》第十四章提出：“视之不见，名曰夷；听之不闻，名曰希；搏之不得，名曰微。此三者不可致诘，故混而为一。”道作为超验本体存在，具有双重不可感知性——既无感官可察的具象显象，亦无形质可循的实体，从根本上突破了人类认知框架的经验边界。首章“道可道，非恒道；名可名，非恒名”的命题深刻揭示语言符号系统在描述本体之道的内在困境：任何概念化的命名必然导致对道之本真状态的对象化遮蔽。这种言说困境源于语言本身的相对性与局限性。对道的把握需要超越逻辑认知范式，转向“观物取象—直觉体认”的非概念化认知路径。作为宇宙本原，道兼摄生成性与超越性双重维度：既呈现为“无中生有”的创生机制，又作为统摄万物的终极依据存在，在“有”“无”辩证运动中维系本体与现象的结构性关联。

《道德经》构建的体道方法以“致虚极，守静笃”（第十六章）的内向性修证为核心，主张通过“涤除玄鉴”（第十章）的心灵净化，实现“不出户，知天下；不窥牖，见天道”（第四十七章）的超验体悟。这种直觉主义认知路径与亚里士多德形而上学的逻辑推演形成范式分野：前者通过消解主客二分的体道实践抵达终极实在，后者依赖理性分析建构存在论体系，二者共同构成了人类探索本体世界的两种元认知范式。

（3）The Linguistic Transcendence of Dao

Chapter 14 of *Dao De Jing* states："Being looked at, yet it cannot be seen. So we call it the Invisible. Being listened to, yet it cannot be heard. So we call it the Inaudible. Being reached for, yet it cannot be touched. So we call it the Intangible. These three cannot be fathomed, and they are thus blended into one." As a transcendental ontological reality, Dao evades dual perception: it lacks sensory manifestations and material substance, fundamentally transcending the empirical boundaries of human cognition. The proposition in Chapter 1—"The Dao that can be spoken of is not the eternal Dao; the name that can be named is not the eternal name"—profoundly exposes the inherent dilemma of linguistic sign systems in describing the ontological Dao: any conceptual naming inevitably objectifies and obscures its authentic state. This linguistic predicament arises from the relativity and limitation of language itself. Grasping Dao requires transcending the logical cognitive paradigm and embracing a non-conceptual cognitive path of "observing things to abstract images—intuitive apprehension". As the cosmic origin, Dao integrates dual dimensions of generativity and transcendence: it manifests as a "being is born from non-being" mechanism while serving as the ultimate ground of all things, maintaining the structural correlation between ontology and phenomena through the dialectical movement of being and non-being."

Dao De Jing advocates an introspective approach to realize Dao: "attain ultimate void, keep extreme stillness" (Chapter 16). Through mental purification of "cleansing the mystic mirror" (Chapter 10), it advocates achieving transcendental insight: "Without going out of doors, one can know the whole world; without looking out of the windows, one can perceive the Dao of Heaven." (Chapter 47). This intuitive cognitive approach contrasts sharply with Aristotle's metaphysical logical deduction: the former realizes ultimate reality by dissolving subject–object duality in praxis, while the latter constructs an ontological system through rational analysis. Together, they constitute two meta-cognitive paradigms of humanity's exploration into ontological reality.

二、道的特性

（一）道的自然无为

“自然”与“无为”构成道的本体论属性。《道德经》第二十五章“道法自然”与第五十一章“恒自然”的命题确立了道的自然本质——此“自然”非实体性自然物，而是指事物自生自化的本然状态，即不受外在意志干预的自主性演化机制。作为宇宙本原，道的创生模式具有内在自发性：其化育万物非依主观意志，而遵循“生而不有，为而不恃”（第五十一章）的客观规律。

“无为”作为“自然”的实践向度，在第三十七章“道恒无为而无不为”中获本体论阐释，本质是摒弃“妄作”（第十六章）的人为干预，以“辅万物之自然”（第六十四章）为准则。这一特性在政治哲学层面具象为圣人治理范式：通过“处无为之事”（第二章）、“好静”（第五十七章）、“希言”（第二十三章）等实践策略，达成“民自化”（第五十七章）的理想状态。《道德经》中十七处相关论述（第二、三、五、十、十七、二十四、二十九、三十七、三十八、四十三、四十八、五十一、五十七、六十三、六十四、七十三、七十五章）形成互文网络，揭示“无为”与“自然”的辩证关系：前者是后者的方法论表达，后者是前者的价值根基。

自然无为原则在政治场域衍生出三重实践逻辑：为政者维度的“不言之教”（第二章）、“守中”（第五章）等因循型治理，社会维度的“自化—自正—自富—自朴”（第五十七章）的内生性秩序，规避“民之难治”（第七十五章）的治理危机预防功能。这种“无为—自然”的双向建构最终指向“功成事遂，百姓皆谓我自然”（第十七章）的治理境界。

Ⅱ. The Characteristics of Dao

(1) Naturalness and "Wu-Wei" (Non-Action) of Dao

Naturalness and "wu-wei" (non-action) constitute Dao's ontological attributes. *Dao De Jing*'s propositions—"the law of Dao is natural" (Chapter 25) and "all following the course of nature" (Chapter 51)—define Dao's self-essence: "naturalness" here does not denote substantial nature but the spontaneous state of things' self-generation and self-transformation, an autonomous evolutionary mechanism free from external volitional interference. As the cosmic origin, Dao's generative model is inherently spontaneous: it nurtures all things not by subjective will but by the objective principle of "creating all things without possessing them, promoting all things without relying its ability" (Chapter 51).

As the practical dimension of "naturalness", "wu-wei" (non-action) receives ontological interpretation in Chapter 37: "Dao never acts with interference, yet there is nothing it cannot do." Its essence is rejecting "arbitrary interference" (Chapter 16) and adhering to the norm of "assisting the natural development of all things" (Chapter 64). In political philosophy, this translates to the sage's governance paradigm: through practices like "managing affairs by means of 'wu-wei' (non-action)" (Chapter 2), "maintaining stillness" (Chapter 57), and "rarely speaking" (Chapter 23), the ideal state of "the people are transformed by themselves" (Chapter 57) is achieved. Seventeen interrelated discourses in *Dao De Jing* (Chapters 2, 3, 5, 10, 17, 24, 29, 37, 38, 43, 48, 51, 57, 63, 64, 73, 75) form an intertextual network, revealing the dialectics of "wu-wei" (non-action) and "naturalness": the former is the methodological expression, and the latter is the axiological foundation.

In the political domain, the principle of naturalness and "wu-wei" (non-action) generates three practical logics: adaptive governance by rulers through "teaching without words" (Chapter 2) and "keeping to the mean" (Chapter 5); endogenous social order of "self-transformation, self-correction, self-enriching, and self-simplicity" (Chapter 57); and crisis prevention by avoiding "the people are difficult to rule" (Chapter 75). This dual construction of "wu-wei" (non-action) – naturalness culminates in the ideal governance state: "When their missions are accomplished and their work done, the people would all remark: 'We are naturally like this'." (Chapter 17)

(二) 道的柔弱不争

柔弱性构成道的实践模态。《道德经》二十余处关于"柔""弱"的论述（第三十六、四十一、四十三、五十二、七十六、七十八章等），揭示其作为道体作用的核心机制——通过"弱者道之用"（第四十章）的潜隐运作，实现"柔弱胜刚强"（第三十六章）的辩证转化。这种弱作用力本质上是道体自然性的延伸：摒弃刚性干预，以水润万物式的渗透性推动宇宙运化，在"天下之至柔，驰骋天下之至坚"（第四十三章）的逆向生成逻辑中维系万物生发。

《道德经》文本通过双重隐喻深化柔弱特质：水意象阐释空间维度（第八、七十八章），展现柔性力量的流动性（随物赋形）与穿透性（滴水穿石）；雌牝意象则揭示其性别维度（第六十一章等），通过"守其雌"（第二十八章）的虚静策略实现"以静胜牡"（第六十一章）的治理效能。二者共同建构"柔弱—刚强"的辩证认知框架：刚性作为"死之徒"（第七十六章）表征生命力的耗散，柔性作为"生之徒"（第七十六章）体现道的生发本质。

不争性作为柔弱特质的外显形态，在政治哲学层面具象为"处下"（第六十六章）、"居后"（第六十六、六十七章）、"曲全"（第二十二章）等实践原则。这种“善下”（第六十六章）的治理智慧，通过江海纳百川（第六十六章）、大国以下小国（第六十一章）等喻象，形成“不争而善胜”（第七十三章）的逆向治理逻辑，本质上是消弭主体逞强好胜的意志，在“为而不争”（第八十一章）的玄同中达成“天下莫能与之争”（第六十六章）的终极治理效果。柔弱与不争互文：前者构成后者的本体依据，后者成为前者的实践路径，共同指向“道法自然”的核心命题，在“守柔曰强”（第五十二章）的辩证思维中完成从宇宙论到政治哲学的范式转换。

（2）Softness and Non-Contention of Dao

Softness defines Dao's practical modality. *Dao De Jing*'s twenty-plus discourses on "softness" and "weakness" (Chapters 36, 41, 43, 52, 76, 78, etc.) reveal its core operational mechanism: through the latent function of "softness and weakness are the functions of Dao" (Chapter 40), it achieves the dialectical transformation of "the soft prevails over the hard" (Chapter 36). This weak force extends Dao's naturalness: eschewing rigid intervention, it propels cosmic operations through water-like permeability, sustaining life in the reverse generative logic of "the softest under Heaven masters the hardest" (Chapter 43).

The text deepens softness through dual metaphors: the water imagery (Chapters 8, 78) explicates the spatial dimension, demonstrating soft power's fluidity (water adapts to forms) and penetrability (water wears stone); the female imagery (Chapter 61, etc.) reveals the gender dimension, achieving governance efficacy of "conquers the masculine by her stillness" (Chapter 61) through the strategy of "keeping to the feminine" (Chapter 28). Together, they construct the "softness - hardness" dialectical framework: hardness, as the "path of death" (Chapter 76), signifies vitality dissipation, while softness, as the "path of life" (Chapter 76), embodies Dao's generative essence.

As the external expression of softness, non-contention materializes in political philosophy as principles of "staying in the lower position" (Chapter 66), "keeping behind" (Chapters 66, 67), and "enduring grievances leading to self-preservation" (Chapter 22). This governance wisdom of "being good at staying in a low position" (Chapter 66)—epitomized by rivers and seas embracing valley streams (Chapter 66) and a large state abasing itself to a small state (Chapter 61)—forms the reverse logic of "being good at winning without contending" (Chapter 73). Its essence lies in eliminating the will to "show off strength and pursue victory", achieving the ultimate governance effect of "no one under Heaven can contend with him" (Chapter 66) through the unity of "acting without contention" (Chapter 81). Softness and non-contention are interwoven: the former is the ontological basis, the latter the practical path, both converging on "the law of Dao is natural". They complete the paradigmatic shift from cosmology to political philosophy through the dialectical logic of "keeping the soft is called power" (Chapter 52).

(三) 道的周行性

周行构成道的运动模态。《道德经》通过"复"(第十六章)、"反"(第四十章)、"周行"(第二十五章)三重范畴,建构"道动"的本体论规定性。其中"反者道之动"(第四十章)作为核心命题,包含双重运作机制:本体维度的"复归其根"(第十六章)——万物通过"观复"(第十六章)回归"静曰复命"(第十六章)的本真状态;现象维度的"逆向生成"—"物壮则老"(第五十五章)揭示物极必反的转化律,而"将欲歙之,必固张之"(第三十六章)展现反向运动的调控策略,共同构成"正反相成"的辩证运动体系。

这种周行性在宇宙生成论中具象为"有无相生"(第二章)的动态平衡结构。通过"有生于无"(第四十章)的生成路径与"复归于无物"(第十四章)的返本路径,形成"无—有—无"的循环本体论模型。道体在此过程中实现双重确证:作为"恒无"(第一章)的本体实在,通过"冲气为和"(第四十二章)的氤氲化生功能创生万物;作为"恒有"(第一章)的显化规律,通过"大曰逝,逝曰远,远曰反"(第二十五章)的时空延展维系宇宙秩序。

周行不殆的运动模态蕴含三重哲学意蕴:通过"复命曰常"(第十六章)确立自然法则恒常性,通过"周行而不殆"(第二十五章)彰显运动过程无限性，通过“祸福相伏”（第五十八章）揭示矛盾转化必然性。这三重维度共同锚定道作为“天地根”（第六章）的终极地位，在循环运动中完成“独立而不改”（第二十五章）的本体论展演。

（3）**Cyclical Movement of Dao**

Cyclical movement defines Dao's modality of motion. *Dao De Jing* constructs the ontological determination of "Dao's movement" through three categories: "return" (Chapter 16), "reversion" (Chapter 40), and "moving in a cycle" (Chapter 25). The core proposition "reversal and cyclical recurrence are the movement of Dao" (Chapter 40) entails a dual mechanism: ontological "returning to the root" (Chapter 16), where all things revert to their authentic state of "stillness is called returning to their destiny" (Chapter 16) through "observing return" (Chapter 16); phenomenological "reverse generation", where "things decline when overly strong" (Chapter 55) embody the law of polar reversal, while "to contract, one must first expand" (Chapter 36) illustrates reverse regulatory strategies, forming a dialectical system of "mutual completion of opposites".

This cyclicality manifests in cosmogony as the dynamic balance of "being and non-being give rise to each other" (Chapter 2), forming a cyclic ontological model of "non-being→being→non-being" through the generative path of "being emerges from non-being" (Chapter 40) and the return path of "reverting to the state of nothingness" (Chapter 14). Dao achieves dual confirmation: as "eternal non-being" (Chapter 1), it generates all things through the harmonious blending of qi; as "eternal being" (Chapter 1), it sustains cosmic order through spatiotemporal extension: "boundless and ceaseless, reaching far away, and returning to its origin" (Chapter 25).

The modality of unceasing cyclical movement carries three philosophical meanings: "returning to their destiny is called the eternal law" (Chapter 16) establishes natural laws' permanence; "moving in a cycle and never ceasing" (Chapter 25) demonstrates movement's infinity; "fortune and misfortune interweave" (Chapter 58) reveals contradictory transformation's necessity. These dimensions anchor Dao's ultimate status as the "root of Heaven and Earth" (Chapter 6), completing its ontological demonstration of "independent and unchanging" (Chapter 25) through cyclical motion.

参考文献

Alexander, G. G. *Lao-Tsze, the Great Thinker, with a Translation of His Thought on Nature and Manifestations of God* [M]. London: Paul, 1895.

Ames, R. T. & Hall, D. L. *Dao De Jing: Making This Life Significant—A Philosophical Translation* [M]. New York: Ballantine, 2004.

Blakney, R. B. & Richard, John Lynn. *DAO TE CHING* [M]. New York: Penguin Group Inc., 2007.

Grossman, R. *The Dao of Emerson: The Wisdom of Dao Te Ching as Found in the Words of Ralph Waldo Emerson* [M]. New York: Modern Library, 2007.

John, C. H. *Dao Teh Ching* [M]. Boston & London: Shambhala, 1990.

John, Heider. *The Dao of Leadership: The Ancient Wisdom of Dao Te Ching* [M]. Atlatas: Humanics Publishing / Green Dragon Publishing Group, 1985.

Lau, D. C. *Tao Te Ching* [M]. Baltimore: Penguin Books, 1963.

Legge, J. *The Texts of Daoism* [M]. New York: Dover Publication, 1962.

Sam, H. *Dao Te Ching, a New Translation* [M]. Boston and London: Shambhala, 2007.

Stephen, M. *Dao Te Ching* [M]. New York: Harper Collins Publishers, 1988.

Waley, A. *The Way and Its Power: The Dao Te Ching and Its Place in Chinese Thought* [M]. New York: Grove Press Inc., 1988.

Wayne, W. Dyer. *Living the Wisdom of the Dao* [M]. Hong Kong: Hay House, 2008.

Wing-tsit, C. *The Way of Lao Tzu (Tao-te Ching)* [M]. New York: Macmillan, 1963.

安乐哲，郝大维. 道不远人：比较哲学视域中的《老子》[M]. 北京：学苑出版社, 2004.

安伦. 理性信仰之道:人类宗教共同体[M]. 上海: 学林出版社, 2009.

安伦. 老子指真[M]. 北京: 社会科学文献出版社, 2016.

陈鼓应. 老子注译及评介[M]. 北京: 中华书局, 2015.

陈鼓应. 老子今注今译[M]. 北京: 中华书局, 2020.

冯友兰. 中国哲学史新编[M]. 北京: 人民出版社,1986.

傅佩荣. 傅佩荣解读老子[M]. 北京: 线装书局, 2006.

高亨. 老子正诂[M]. 北京: 清华大学出版社, 2011.

高明. 帛书老子校注[M]. 北京: 中华书局, 2018.

辜正坤. 新编老子道德经: 汉英对照[M]. 北京: 外语教学与研究出版社, 2022.

胡适. 中国哲学史大纲[M]. 北京: 东方出版社, 2004.

蒋锡昌. 老子校诂[M]. 上海: 上海书店, 1988.

卡尔·雅斯贝斯. 历史的起源与目标[M]. 魏楚雄, 俞新天, 译. 北京: 华夏出版社, 1989.

老子. 道德经: 中英对照[M]. 刘殿爵, 译. 北京: 中国对外翻译出版公司, 2012.

老子. 道德经: 汉英对照[M]. 安伦, 译. 上海: 上海交通大学出版社, 2021.

李约瑟. 中国古代科学思想史[M]. 陈立夫, 等译. 南昌: 江西人民出版社, 1990.

梁漱溟. 东西文化及其哲学[M]. 北京: 商务印书馆, 2021.

林语堂. 老子的智慧[M]. 西安: 陕西师范大学出版社, 2006.

刘笑敢. 老子古今[M]. 北京: 中国社会科学出版社, 2006.

马叙伦. 老子校诂[M]. 北京: 中华书局, 1974.

苗力田. 亚里士多德选集[M]. 北京: 中国人民大学出版社, 2000.

牟钟鉴. 老子新说[M]. 北京: 商务印书馆, 2021.

任继愈. 老子新译[M]. 上海: 上海古籍出版社, 1978.

斯宾诺莎. 简论上帝、人及其心灵健康[M]. 顾寿观, 译. 北京: 商务印书馆, 2017.

王弼. 道德真经注[M]. 北京: 中华书局, 2011.

王德峰．哲学导论［M］．上海：上海人民出版社，2000.

王德峰．艺术哲学［M］．上海：复旦大学出版社，2005.

吴雪萌．英语世界老学研究［M］．武汉：华中师范大学出版社，2016.

辛红娟．《道德经》在英语世界［M］．上海：上海译文出版社，2007.

许抗生．帛书老子注释与研究［M］．杭州：浙江人民出版社，1985.

许慎．说文解字［M］．长春：吉林美术出版社，2015.

许渊冲．道德经：汉英对照［M］．北京：五洲传播出版社、中华书局，2018.

杨丙安．老子古本合校［M］．北京：中华书局，2014.

杨鹏．道德经：汉英对照［M］．北京：新世界出版社，2019.

杨义．老子还原［M］．北京：中华书局，2011.

俞森林．道经英译史［M］．上海：上海三联书店，2020.

俞樾．诸子平议［M］．南京：凤凰出版社，2020.

曾仕强．曾仕强详解道德经：道经［M］．北京：民主与建设出版社，2016.

曾仕强．曾仕强详解道德经：德经［M］．北京：民主与建设出版社，2016.

张岱年．中国哲学大纲［M］．北京：中国社会科学出版社，1982.

张其成．张其成全解道德经［M］．北京：华夏出版社，2017.

张松辉．老子研究［M］．北京：人民出版社，2009.

张松如．老子校读［M］．长春：吉林人民出版社，1981.

章媛．《道德经》西传之云变［M］．北京：中国社会科学出版社，2021.

朱俊红．《道德经》四帝注［M］．海口：海南出版社，2012.

朱谦之．老子校释［M］．北京：中华书局，1984.